HUNGER AND DREAMS

The Alaskan Women's Anthology
Edited by Patricia Monaghan
Illustrated by Jan Leone

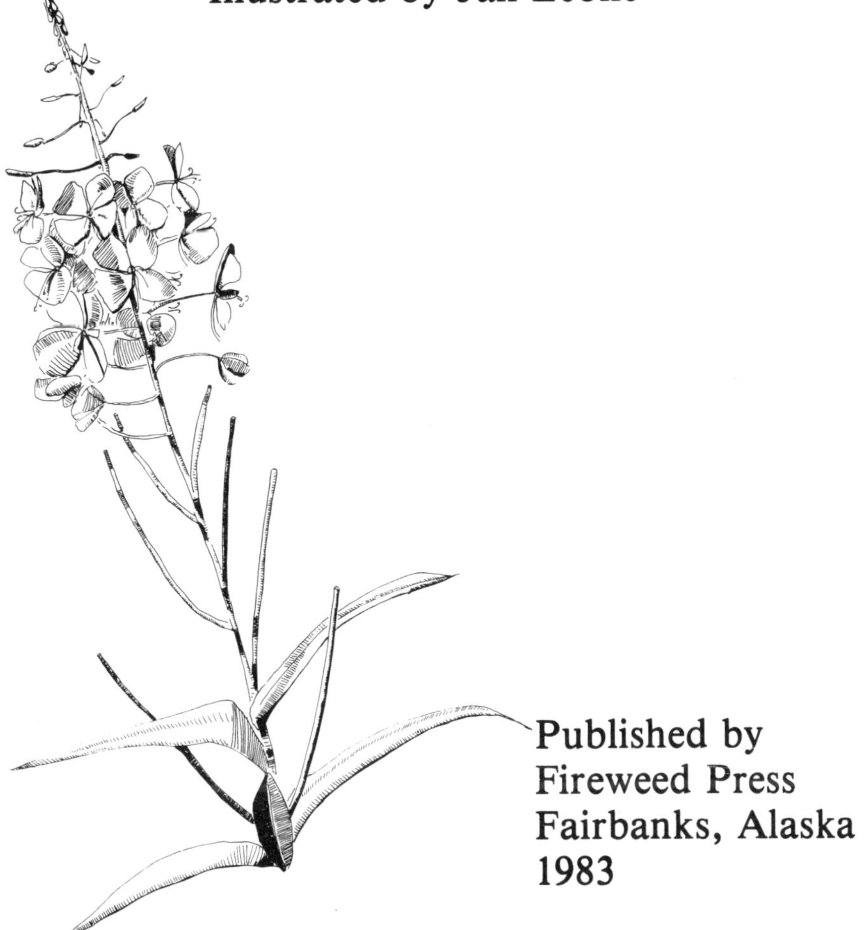

Published by
Fireweed Press
Fairbanks, Alaska
1983

FIRST EDITION

ISBN: 0-914221-00-0

ACKNOWLEDGEMENTS

Many Alaskans have helped in the production of this book, of whom the following deserve special thanks: Eva Bee for typesetting; Larry Laraby of Spirit Mountain Press for design assistance; Bridget Smith of Firsthand Press for promotional aid; and Jane Pender for proofreading.

In addition, the following women, through their contributions, paid for the first printing: Jean Anderson, Carol Gold, Suzanne Iudicello, Lisa Rudd, Charla Ranch, and Evelyn Wiszinckas.

TABLE OF CONTENTS

Patricia Monaghan
INTRODUCTION

In Alaska, literature has primarily been the occupation of
the male traveller. Robert Service, Jack London, John Muir,
Norman Mailer, John McPhee, each has come to Alaska
briefly to test himself against the arctic.

Test himself as a person, against the land; test himself as a
writer, against the subject, "The Last Frontier" standing to
the twentieth century as the earlier frontier did to the nine-
teenth. Alaska is a subject for the ambitious young writer to
exploit for a first book, one for the established writer to take
on when he needs something worthy of his talent. And so
this century has brought us the beginnings of an Alaskan
literary tradition: white men come and make anew those
observations each newcomer makes, that the land has a stern
magic, that vast distances and slanting light affect even your
dreams, that people here live on edges not as accessible to
those in more temperate climes.

But many are outside this tradition. We are women,
Native Alaskans, men who make homes here. For us, there
is another, minor tradition: nature writing. John Haines
stands as a fine example of a poet who has found a home

within that tradition, but popular journalism of the Alaska Magazine variety stems from it too.

In either type of writing, however, Alaska does not stand at the center of its literature, but is in a paradoxical way peripheral to it. The real center of literature is "Outside," for Alaska remains an artistic province, a colony. Writers presume their readership is elsewhere and so direct their words. The result: sometimes over-explanatory or defensive ("we've got to get *them* to see it *our* way"), sometimes sensational ("you wouldn't believe what goes on") and sometimes, perhaps most often, simply trite ("Alaska is the largest state").

When people, rather than landscapes, are the subject, the limitations of both available traditions become particularly clear. The Outside writer sees only a season of a community's life; the nature writer by definition must ignore it. As a result, most literature is pastoral, reminiscent of those works of London poets visiting the countryside to find inspiration among the shepherdesses. Or it is anti-pastoral, disgusted at the lives of the rude peasant. On the one hand, Dryden's "cruel nymph" Phyllis; on the other, Jonathan Swift's revolting Chloe, Wycherly's laughable Country Wife. Yeats, seeing a similar division affecting Irish literature before his day, condemned the exploitation of his land as "buffoonery and easy sentiment."

But as a literature matures — as it produces a Thomas Hardy, a Willa Cather — a new tradition emerges. Ireland, early in this century, transformed its literature from a London-based to a Dublin-based, then to a truly national literature. Poet Patrick Kavanaugh described the difference as between a "provincial" literature, written from the provinces to the capital and always aware of the inferior status of the former; and a "parochial" literature, written from the parish to anyone, anywhere, truly interested in the doings of the parish. Using Kavanaugh's definition, we can see in Alaskan literature to date a primarily provincial attitude.

But a new voice, what Kavanaugh would call a parochial one, has begun to emerge. The poems and stories in this book speak in it. The result of a 1981 search for work by and about Alaskan women, this collection speaks clearly Alaskan life. Nature exists here, but as a place to live, not merely to visit. The people who exist here are neither noble savages and innocent shepherdesses, nor rakes and ruffians. The Alaska in this book is a land of hunger and dreams, and the women who live here are survivors of both.

HUNGER

Katherine McNamara
FISH STORY

Old lady fishes
Baits her hook with words
All day talks fish
Through a hole in the ice
End of the day
Sets a spruce bush in the hole
Packs her story home

Bridget A. Smith
THE SNARE

Soon after I arrived in Ophir, Belle showed me how to snare rabbits.
She told me that fresh meat was important in winter, and besides, I had
to learn how to take care of myself. I told her I had done just fine for
38 years without snaring rabbits.

We were about two miles from Ophir, an abandoned mining town on
the banks of a tributary of the Yukon. Belle had lived in Ophir on and
off since she was a young girl — then it had been a living town with a
library, operahouse, three churches, and a roadhouse. Now, living
among the ruins of the log buildings, she was a relic among relics.

She bent down with difficulty to point out the distinctive tracks
zigzagging through the snow. "See there. Rabbits like to chew on these
green shoots." Tiny paths twisted in and around the slim willows and
brown pellets signaled the presence of her prey. From her jacket
pocket, Belle took a piece of wire, already shaped into a noose, and at-
tached it with string to the shoots so that it hung directly in the path.

"I don't understand how it works," I said.

"The rabbit just comes along here, its head gets caught in the noose
which tightens, and it dies."

I could just see the white furry animal, scampering about like Peter
Rabbit, and then, struggling in the wire.

"Does it kill quickly?" I asked doubtfully.

"Depends on you, honey. Do it right, they won't suffer."

I had no intention of making them suffer, much less snaring them. I would make do with canned meat. Her whole demonstration made me feel queasy.

Belle was silent on the way back; she snowshoed, I skied. She was breathing hard, even though it was level ground. Reaching her cabin, she invited me in for coffee. She poured it into thick white mugs from the pot on the back of the woodstove, and sank down heavily across from me. While her breathing slowly eased, I looked around her cabin.

The log walls were barely 7 feet high; covering one entire wall were hundreds of ancient copies of the Congressional Digest stacked up, one on top of another, "for insulation," she had said. On another wall were photographs of people she had known — most of them dead now. During one visit, she had taken me over to her "rogues' gallery" and told stories about each one of the faces staring out of the heavy frames.

In a corner, an orange and red quilt covered her bed which was elevated 10 inches from the floor, as was a purple overstuffed sofa. "I leave 'em like that all the time," she had told me, as protection against the regular spring flooding. Those books and magazines not crammed into bookcases were stacked neatly on the planked floor. Rocks, bits of dried plants, bones, and some unidentifiable objects covered every surface in the place. Only the kitchen table where we sat was clear.

After her breathing had eased, she spoke. "I'm eighty years old, Maggie, and going into the final stretch." I opened my mouth to protest, to say she had many years left, but she waved away the unspoken words. "Next spring, I'm checking into the Pioneer Home in Fairbanks. Some of my friends are there — even one of my ex-husbands." She winked at me. "This is my last winter here and I need your help."

I knew what was coming. Belle was going to ask me to snare rabbits; just the thought filled me with revulsion. But how could I refuse her?

"I need fresh meat," she said. My heart sank. "Oh, I could live without it," she continued, "but I like it and it makes me feel strong." I couldn't say anything. She looked down at her gnarled hands. "I'm too old and tired to snare them anymore."

There she was, sitting up so straight, bright brown eyes, impossibly dark hair, cherry red sweater. She didn't look too old and tired. But I had heard her labored breathing. My reply was very tentative. "Well, I guess I could give it a try."

She clapped her hands and almost skipped to the cupboard to get a bottle of whiskey and two shot glasses decorated with the map of Alaska in primary colors. After filling them to the brim, she lifted hers, saying, "Here's to our partnership," and drank it down. I lifted mine

in return with a weak "Cheers" and sipped cautiously. The warmth of
the whiskey didn't make me feel any better. I was a sculptor — not a
killer — of animals. I would check the snare once and then tell her I
couldn't do it anymore.

As I skied home that night down the once lively main street of Ophir,
a light snow was falling. On each side of me, dark log buildings leaned
towards one another; mine was one of the few which didn't. Inside, I
studied the bleak place I had chosen to spend the winter. On a rusty
old bedstead in the corner, my tapered down sleeping bag didn't quite
cover the narrow stained mattress. Except for a 1957 calendar and a
few nails, the log walls were bare. A table and two wooden chairs com-
pleted the meager furnishings. My mother would have begun decorating
immediately. When she died, every piece of furniture in her downtown
Anchorage condominium was highly polished French Provincial. A
mammoth armoire she had converted to a display case dominated the
livingroom. In it, she exhibited the soapstone sculptures I made for her
— three every year — at Christmas, on her birthday, and on Mother's
Day. Whenever I found an unusual piece of stone, I would set it aside
for her, rather than using it for the carvings I sold to retail stores in
town. Once a week, when I came to town to deliver the carvings, I
would meet her for lunch at a downtown restaurant dressed in Army
Surplus cottons or woolens, depending on the season. She wore elegant
silk or wool suits made especially for her, and carried a leather handbag
out of which slipped a creamy envelope containing $50.00, which found
its way across the table before coffee.

We talked about ordinary things. Our lives touched only at our
weekly lunches and an occasional dinner in her home. She rarely ven-
tured to my dog-filled cabin, preferring instead to imagine me in more
conventional surroundings. She was the only one who called me
"Margaret" believing that "Maggie" sounded like an Irish maid. Her
death after a stroke made me feel isolated and alone. Coming to Ophir
for the winter had been a decision made without thought, a longing for
direction translated into movement.

Shivering, I slipped into the clammy sleeping bag, remembering where
I would be going the next day. I went to sleep, hoping that no small
animal had found its way to the snare.

The next day, the winter sun was just beginning to skim the horizon
by the time I finished coffee and oatmeal. It took longer than usual to
bank the fire in the woodstove and adjust the draft. The thermometer
outside the tiny window registered 10 below. The bare little cabin ac-
tually looked inviting.

Covered with down, I walked outside where, under a gray sky, I
fumbled with the thick leather fastenings on the skis. Once I began

moving in my own glazed tracks, I became warm, even though I skied very slowly, willing all rabbits to stay away from the snare. By the time I reached the willows where we had been the day before, some escaping hairs around the edge of my hat were frosted white — the same color as the small plump ghost half suspended by the wire. I didn't want to touch him. Leaning on the poles, I grew steadily colder looking at him hanging in the willows. Struggling to keep the nausea down, I squatted down, and stretched out both hands to pull him toward me. But Belle had set the snare well. I had to take off one glove to slip the noose off his soft neck before he could be placed gently into my pack. Even when he was out of sight, I could still see him, head bent humbly. I promised myself that I would tell Belle as soon as I returned that I could do it no more.

When I presented the rabbit to her, she began moving quickly around the kitchen making preparations. Newspapers appeared on the kitchen table as well as several sharp knives with thick wooden handles. While I watched, she skinned the animal deftly — it looked so vulnerable without its fur.

Her eyes were bright when she looked up from her work. "Come back for dinner, Maggie. We're having fried rabbit with gravy." The last thing I wanted to do was to eat the rabbit, but I didn't want to spoil her happy mood so nodded as I moved toward the door. "Take that with you," she said, pointing to a yellow bundle. "It's just gathering dust here." She turned back to her task, humming softly as she wielded the knife with bloody hands. The dust catcher was a heavy sun-colored quilt, intricately worked.

At home, the quilt glowed softly on my bed. My mother would have liked it. Still thinking of her, I took out a soapstone carving I had been working on and spent the afternoon finishing it. It made me forget that I still had to tell Belle that I couldn't snare anymore.

By dinnertime, the yellow light of the kerosene lantern reflected off the curves of the plump green rabbit as I polished it with a soft cloth. Slipping it into my pocket, I skied to Belle's to be greeted with the savory aroma of meat. I handed her the soapstone carving, saying, "For you, Belle." She took it cautiously and carried it slowly over to the lantern, turning it over and over. She carefully placed it on the table and walked over to the stove, still looking at it. She switched her steady gaze to me for the first time since I had handed her the figure. "It's beautiful, Margaret. It looks so real." Then she gave a final stir to the dark brown gravy and asked me to pull up a chair.

I helped myself to one of the smaller pieces of the crisp rabbit, a biscuit, a spoonful of gravy and some peas. She watched me cut the meat into tiny pieces. The first one I swallowed whole, holding my breath, expecting my stomach to heave. The second I washed down

with water, still waiting for some physical reaction. Nothing happened.
The third bite I chewed a few times very tentatively before washing it
down. The taste was beginning to come through. Instead of feeling
repugnance, my mouth was actually watering. I was looking forward to
the next bite. "It's good," I exclaimed with surprise. Belle was amused.
 "Course it is. I don't like it for nothing."

After dinner, we leaned back in our chairs, drinking coffee and listen-
ing to the hiss of the lantern. It was the perfect time for telling Belle of
my reluctance to snare rabbits but somehow the words weren't there. It
occurred to me that the contentment on her face as she held the
soapstone rabbit on her aproned lap was an expression I wanted to see
for the rest of the winter.

Sheila Nickerson
NEIGHBOR

Suppose that old woman—
I have seen her once—
Living in that small green house
Is related to raspberries.
They alone climb up her walk
Every spring and reach till
They can peek in the windows.
I have seen no one—
Not even dog or pigeon—
Go up that path
In any season. And suppose
That she dies in winter
And that is why her path
Is never cleared of snow
And that she rises in spring
With red sap, a vision,
To be met at the door
By her cousins coming for summer.
They carry small bags packed tight,
They gossip like mad.
Leaning against each other,
They dress up,
They whisper of red,
They dream of sleep that follows fruit.
And suppose that we
Opened her door in winter
And saw her there,
A tiny nest of roots.

Mary TallMountain
THE HANDS OF MARY JOE

for my mother, an Athabaskan woman

Her hands lift and tend King Salmon
Cherish the skin of her child
Light as willow-buds
Thread a needle's invisible eye
In dim flickering lamplight
Fingers weave patterns
In violet and amber beads

The brown-pearl hands
Etched with tiny lines
Curled into little cups
Stiffened, yet with
Delicate touch
Draw a comb of tortoise shell
Through dark-silvered hair

Hands that flowed in rhythms
Smooth as riverdrift
Attuned to daily music
Of her hidden life
Now lie folded in her lap
Trembling minutely
The hands of Mary Joe
Await
The approaching silence

Joanne Townsend
LEAVETAKING

I gather the late peas.
How the wind has snapped the tall vines!
They lean bent as an old man's failed back
in the direction of the cornflowers
and those stubborn cornflowers
their fringed faces more violet than blue
keep blooming
as if to deny chill in the air,
the thinning of light,
fresh snow on the mountain.
Short hours from death they pulse
like notes from Delius' English Rhapsody,
and this land, this shaman that holds me,
throbs too, alive under my feet.
True, the water rushes towards its season of ice,
the leaves fly from the birch,
the tourists and I make our reservations,
but before the goodbyes, while there is still
the one bud on the wild rose,
Spirit Woman will rise from these furrows.
She burns like fireweed.
She is strong as seal gut.
She is plump from salmonberries.
"Here is the map," she will say
and wind her hair into rings of tree.

Linda Green
ANNIE

Deeply lined, this face of Raven clan.
Eyes alive with magic,
Though not carefree.
She bore the changes of her people.

    In dim light she worked, worked swiftly
    Those fingers . . .
    overlay, warp — weft, twist.
    As rotting teeth held the roots with tension.
    Oh, the shiny white roots
    long and slim, easy to weave.
    Gathered at favorite spots.
    Cooked by Matthew on the beach.

And in the evenings, when she told
the tales of Tlingit ways
Of weavings, baskets, and more . . .
I was intrigued,
enchanted.
Connected, somehow.

Afterward I went to see Matthew
Knowing she would like that.
Wishing I could care about his words.
Feeling only emptiness as he spoke of her,
showed pictures of her.

    They said a shaman cast a spell.
    And now her eyes shut tight
    Never to show secrets reflected.

M. Lindholm
THE POACHING

"We sure could use the meat, Lindy." Mom's voice was hopeful as a child's but the trace of urgency in it was entirely adult.

The Sir continued to stare out the darkened kitchen window. That was the first thing Mom had done; as soon as she had noticed the moose moving through the frozen snow that overlay the garden acre, she had snapped out the lights within the house. The darkness had flowed in to replace the glow of a normal evening. The hum of homework, the whine of the small boys arguing together had been silenced. Mom and The Sir stood at the kitchen window, heads together as they peered out around the blanket-curtain. Dell stood at one of the side-windows, where the view was not as good. About her in the darkness she sensed her siblings. Sarah and Sonya had remained at the table, still sitting before their darkened books. Dismay emanated from them, and abject hope that the moose would move on before they caused an inconvenience. But George stood behind her, looking out over her head. Little Mark began to whine. He couldn't see.

"Sssh," Dell hushed him, and made a place in front of her for him to stand. Johnny, too, wrangled his way in front of her. Dell scowled in the dark, but held her peace. All was silent now within the house, awaiting The Sir's decision.

"Neighbors are awful close," he said at last. Need had over-ruled the il-legality of taking moose out of season. There was only the question of feasibility to consider.

The lights of the next house, less than an acre distant, shone like stars through the trees. The neighbors seemed closer now, in the dead of the Fairbanks winter. The leaves of the birches and willows that in summers screened them away were long fallen; the privacy of the log house on Davis Road violated by this evidence of other people.

"A moose would do us through this winter," Mom pointed out shyly. "And it's not like they haven't heard shots before from here. They don't come when we shoot the squirrels anymore."

Dell put her fingertips on the line of fiberglas chinking between two logs. The chill of the winter night reached through the insulation to touch her. The silence was as deep as the darkness. They waited.

The Sir finally spoke.

"Phil, there's a hell of a lot of difference between the sound of a .22 and a 30-40 Krag. And that's what I think I'd better use."

In the darkness Dell breathed again. The decision had been made. Mom was pleased. She was the one who had bought the 30-40, at a junk sale at one of the neighbors. She had got it for twenty dollars. Mom knew little about rifles, but had bought it for The Sir because it seemed like such a good price, and the wooden stock looked well cared for. The Sir had been both astonished and pleased with her. And now it would bring them meat.

The Sir turned away from the window, and the children instinctively stiffened. Battle stations.

"Johnny and Mark. Take the dogs into the basement and stay there with them. I don't want old Bruno getting worked up over a rifle shot, and I sure as hell don't want them barking once it's down. The rest of you get bundled up. Phil, where's that flashlight?"

There was no need to prepare the rifle. It was kept, as every rifle should be, leaning up beside the door, always loaded and always sighted in. For, "What the hell use is an unloaded rifle?" The Sir would de-mand, if all was not as it should be. "You expect me to club someone with it, maybe?"

Dell dressed in the darkness. They all did. They were also silent. At first sight of the moose, when Mom had plunged them all into darkness, The Sir had commanded silence. Only from the basement did vague noises rise, the anxious voices of the little boys in the darkness, the puzzled rustling of the dogs. The darkness and silence made little sense to Dell. The moose had approached the house when it was lit and hum-ming with life. Why would they be spooked now? But it was not her place to make such decisions, or even to voice such a question.

Dell fumbled with extra socks, pulled on a pair of worn out jeans over the ones she already wore. She did not touch her cloth school coat hanging on the wall. Instead she bundled into an old sweater, and then submerged herself in an army surplus parka. Two pairs of mittens, a wool hat, and pull the hood up well over that; she was ready now for the outside climate. Fairbanks had chosen their first winter in Alaska to set some new record lows. Outside it was forty-five degrees below zero. The numbers meant little to Dell. What she did understand was the pinch of nose hairs frozen together, the crimping of eyes when lashes closed in a blink stuck together, of numb feet that tingled painfully when stomped. Fairbanks had already taught her much about cold, in its own swiftly unforgiving way.

"Leave the door open, dammit!" The Sir hissed at George. A wave of condensation was flowing into the house through the open door. Dell moved between George and The Sir. George, tall for his sixteen years, had stiffened at his father's tone. Silently Dell prayed that he would not go off into one of his morose silences. She had read somewhere that fathers and eldest sons always tormented one another. But not tonight, she prayed, not tonight.

The Sir came to the rescue, sensing that George was offended.

"I'm going to stand within the porch when I shoot, almost still inside the front door. I'm hoping that the house will act as a sort of silencer, to swallow up the sound of the shots. Now you point that light just like I told you, and don't waver."

The danger of schism had been averted, at least for tonight. As a unit they moved silently through the opened door. Sarah and Sonya, still only half dressed for the cold, made no move to follow. There would be cold, they knew, and blood and heavy work in the snow. They wanted no part of this. Dell slipped past them without a glance. It wasn't their fault; they had just grown up wrong. If the family had stayed in California, perhaps she would be just like them, worried about boys and cotillions and makeup and clothes. But for Alaska, perhaps the spirit of the night and the kill would not move within her. Dell made no sound as she trod the flimsy boards of the porch. Her father sensed her, and sent her a glare, but she merely huddled the deeper into her parka, literally disappearing within the mound of clothing she wore. He would forget her soon enough.

Her eyes sought the prey. It was always amazing to Dell, just how much she could see in the blackness of a Fairbanks night. It was as if the stars and moon put out more light to make up for the sun's laziness. Or perhaps the snow gave back their faint light to them in a continual exchange.

There was no color to the scene. There were only shades of grey and black. The moose were great blacker shapes against the darkness, blotting out the trees and snows behind them. They seemed to be in a

stupor of cold. They lifted their long legs high above the frozen crust on
the snow when they moved. But they did not move much. For the most
part they stood still in the snow, gazing with long looks of stupidity and
miserable cold at nothing. Only one seemed busy at all. He dug with
methodical pawings at the frozen crust and powdery snow layer that
overlay the cabbage patch. A chunk of frozen stalk and a few leaves
were churned to the top of the snow. Dell listened to his teeth munch
the frozen vegetable. He would be the target. She knew it as firmly as if
The Sir had said it. For the other two were a cow and last spring's calf.
The one chewing was, perhaps, an older calf. No matter. He would be
the one.

Dell focused herself at him. She could feel her father taking aim, even
before George clicked on the light. The light was merely insurance. The
shot would be from The Sir's eyes as much as from the rifle.

The target raised its head, lifting its muzzle from the snow. If any of
the beasts sensed them there, felt the death crouching on that porch,
they did not indicate it. The cow and the calf stood. The prey raised its
head higher, spread the ridiculous Mickey Mouse ears.

The spot light hit it. The silhouette became abruptly a living animal.
Ice rimed its muzzle whiskers, outlined its drooping nose in frost. One
shining black eye threw back the light of the torch even as there was a
great roar next to Dell's ear. The pain of the sound numbed her, until
she was aware of nothing but the ringing in her ears. The sound froze
the moment, outlined it with a faint echo. The beast was down. One
shot. It didn't rise, didn't twitch. The flash flicked out. Silence rushed
back in. The three on the porch didn't stir. The frozen air of the night
swirled behind them back into the house, making huge ghosts of mist
within the comparative warmth of the house. But the three on the porch
waited silently, watching the lights of the neighbors, straining their ears
for some sounds of investigation.

There were none. Perhaps the people were merely uncurious, perhaps
they deemed it wiser not to investigate a single shot in the midst of a
black Fairbanks night. The Sir reached back behind them, pulled the
door shut.

They stepped from the porch into the night. The deep snow of mid-
winter crunched and squeaked under their boots. The cow was moving
now to investigate the fallen one. She snuffled at him curiously as he lay
crumpled in the snow. But she showed no alarm, made no move to flee.

"Cold's made 'em stupid," muttered The Sir. He advanced on his kill
without fear, his rifle in one hand, the flashlight in the other.

"Move along now, there. Shoo! Get along, now!" He moved in on
the curious cow. She stood over last year's calf, not protecting him, but
puzzling over him. The Sir advanced, Dell on his heels and George just
to one side.

"Move along now!" No one disobeyed The Sir when he took that
tone. The cow flapped her incongruous ears, then began a slow retreat.
The Sir reached out, tapped her gently with the flashlight to hasten her.
Finally, she took alarm. With the smaller calf in tow, she moved off
through the deep snow, her long legs rising and falling like hairy
pistons. Even so, it was a good three minutes before they were lost to
sight amongst the trees. They had headed toward the deep woods, not
towards the neighbors. That was good. No one would spot the two and
speculate about a single shot in the night.

The Sir stepped up to the great head of the fallen beast, seized it in
one mittened hand and stretched its throat. Dell had not seen him un-
sheathe the great knife, had not even known he had it. But she would
have been surprised if he had not taken the final step to make certain of
the swift death he had visited upon this creature. There was no spurt of
blood, no sudden flood, but merely a puddling of darkness upon the
snow. The moose was dead, its heart stilled, and already it was begin-
ning to stiffen in the great cold that pressed down upon them all.

Only a tiny plume of steam rose from the rifle wound in its neck, a
smudge of frost already forming about the slash on the throat, to in-
dicate the warmth that still ebbed within the dead animal. The Sir stood
over it, looking down at it a little sadly. "Just meat now," he said at
last. Dell had no reply. George shifted his feet in the snow. "Well,"
The Sir went on in a businesslike tone. "Let's get to work."

Yet all three stood there for a few moments more. For the first time
in her eleven years of life, Dell sensed The Sir at a loss as to what to
do. The moose was bigger dead than alive. And it didn't look like meat
to Dell. It looked like a large dead body. The air was too cold to smell
anything, but she fancied that her nostrils sensed the warmth ebbing
away from the great body. Somehow the releasing of the heat from the
body meant death to Dell, far more so than the losing of its blood.

"First thing," said The Sir at last, as if no time had passed, "Is to
gut it. Then we have to get it cut into quarters and under cover to hang,
so the meat can bleed. Dell, you take the flashlight. George, go get
those knives your mother said she would sharpen. And tell Sonya and
Sarah to get their asses out here and help."

George was gone, crunching through the snow the two hundred or so
feet to the house. The lights inside the house had gone back on, and it
presented its normal aspect to the curious who might peep from
neighboring windows. The door opened to let out light and admit
George. A moment later it re-opened to expel Sonya and Sarah into the
cold and snow. They wandered over disconsolately, to stand huddled
and apart from the great dead animal. The Sir took no note of their ob-
vious dismay at being there.

Obligingly, the animal had fallen more or less on its side. Dell stood still and silent, considering it. The flashlight in her hand was dark. As yet it wasn't needed; no sense in showing a light in the middle of the field for someone to wonder about.

The long legs stuck out at all angles. Drawn by some half knowledge Dell had not known she possessed, she advanced to the beast. She reached down, and seized one of the long hind legs at just above the hoof. She tugged at it gently, feeling the resistance of its weight and the thickening rigor mortis. She heard George return with the knives.

"It will probably be easier to lift if you take it on your shoulder," suggested The Sir. And Dell understood. She stooped, and got her shoulder under the long hock. Then she heaved up, to stand nearly erect under the weight. Now the moose's vulnerable under body lay exposed to the butchers. George and The Sir closed in on it. George took the flashlight from Dell. She was left standing in the dark, the weight of the dead moose's leg upon her shoulder, its coarse fur next to her face. George and The Sir huddled close to the moose's crotch in a circle of light.

"In there, first." "Be careful you don't cut the gut sack." "Go slow!" "Tough hide, huh?" It was a dialogue of vultures and Dell could not distinguish whose voice was which. More steam arose, and carried to her nose a new smell, a smell of death and raw guts and stillborn manure. She gagged a little, silently, lest any mark it. Sarah and Sonya still stood apart, huddled together. The Sir rocked back on his heels, pointed at them with a bloody knife.

"Sonya! Get a bowl or something to put the liver and heart in. Sarah! See if you can find another flashlight. We could use some more light here." They were gone almost before his words were done, grateful to be returning to the warmth of the house, if only for a few minutes.

The cold was beginning to finger Dell. It insinuated itself up the back of her shirt, crept into her boots. With her free hand she moved a scarf up in front of her nose and mouth. In a matter of minutes it was damp and frosty, a discomfort against her face. She twisted her mouth and nose away from it, to have the cold seize her face even tighter. The corners of her eyes were sticking together every time she blinked. The hair inside her nose had turned to tiny prickling ice pins. She did not complain. She would wait a few minutes more. She flexed her mittened hands, felt the foreign tingling in her finger tips. She could wait a little longer.

They were rolling the gut sack out and away from the body, heedless of the blood and slime their mittened hands encountered.

"Good!" grunted The Sir. Dell could tell he was breathing through his mouth, and she knew why. "Didn't puncture it. The meat shouldn't be tainted. Where's Sonya with the bowl?"

The door of the house opened and Sonya hastened toward them with

Sarah in her wake. They scuttled guiltily across the snow as if aware
they had been summoned. Dell saw the bowl bob in Sonya's hands as it
received a weight of flopping steaming liver, had the heart flipped onto
the top of it. She also saw the change that came over Sonya's face when
she had to stand close to the dead moose, and watched her haste as she
returned to the house. Poor Sonya. Only boys and makeup and dances.
No night forces rippling through her, no love-hate for the deep colds
and darks of the Alaska winter. Poor empty Sonya.

The Sir took the flashlight from Sarah's hand, gave her in return a
bundle of knives. Already they needed sharpening. They had never been
intended for this kind of butchery. With something of longing Dell
watched Sarah disappear into the light and warmth of the house. Her
own thighs had a tingling, itching sensation that she well knew was the
forerunner of frostbite.

The Sir remembered her. "Dell, you can let that leg down now. Mind
you don't step in the guts. Go get the wheelbarrow, if you can. Those
guts will have to be disposed of. Can't have the dogs dragging them
around for the world to see."

Dell was grateful to let the leg drop. She stood erect once more, sur-
prised at how good it felt, and at how much weight she had supported
for so long. The moose was looking less like a moose now. The removal
of the guts had hollowed it out like a chocolate Easter bunny. Dell
moved off to find the wheelbarrow. It was, she knew, leaning up
against the logs of the house. And she also knew it hadn't been moved
in three months.

It was buried in snow and frozen to the ground. Dell wasted no time
with a shovel, but merely stomped and shoved the snow aside to get at
it. She reached up to seize the wooden handles, tugged and rocked and
tugged again until finally the ice and frozen mud gave up their grip on
the lip of the wheelbarrow.

The single wheel on it was worse than useless. It would not turn, but
only jammed in the loose snow. Dell ended up dragging it through the
snow by one wooden handle, with the barrow portion half over on its
side. She doubted its usefulness, but it wouldn't do to question The
Sir's use of tools. If he decided it wasn't right for the job, she could put
it back. But the decision wasn't her department.

Back at the moose, there were visible signs of progress. The head had
been mutilated to facilitate the removal of the tongue. It had then been
severed from the body and added to the gut pile. Dell dragged the
wheelbarrow up next to it, and righted it close by. George and The Sir
paid no attention to her. Sarah and Sonya had not returned. Dell knew
they would not.

Dell knew that soon she too would have to go in and get warm. But
she didn't want to be the first to give in. George and The Sir panted in

the cold now, trying vainly not to draw the freezing stuff directly into their lungs. Their voices were muted, as if the icy air were a blanket spread over them, muffling their words. George's voice was a gentle mumble. The Sir's a mellow growl. There was no question of skinning the meat out. They would leave the hide on for now. What remained to be done was to divide the carcass into pieces small enough for them to haul into the secrecy of the garage, there to hang from the rafters and drip dark blood onto the floor beneath.

"We need a saw," asserted George.

"And an axe," growled The Sir, "and rope to hang it by. And I need a cup of coffee. Come on, let's go inside and find out what time it is."

It seemed wrong somehow for all three of them to turn their backs on the dead beast in the snow and hasten toward the lights. It seemed to Dell that something so pagan and huge as the dead moose should have some vigil over it, some guard over its immense death. But the cold pushed her away from that thought and toward the warmth of the log house.

Dell was first at the door, to jerk it open against the barrier of ice that always formed across the bottom. The warmth billowed out about her, somehow making her colder. Once inside, she moved out of the way of the door, and then shouldered out of her heavy coat and kicked her boots off. She was surprised to see that they were fouled with blood and slime, covered with a layer of snow. The blood became real here in the house, where one could see its true color, smell its smell. The dogs, up from the basement, clustered about her, aprickle at the smell of the kill. Bruno's old eyes caught a flash of light and glowed a lambent green at her. Dell smiled at him, a promise of bones.

George and The Sir were behind her, blowing and stamping the cold from their bodies. Mom looked up from the table full of knives she was sharpening.

"We won't need those tonight," The Sir informed her. "I'll be doing the best I can just to get it under cover tonight. And the kids have school tomorrow."

Mom nodded, left off her task to rise from the table. "Do you want me out there to give you a hand?" In voicing the question she was asking to be spared the toil. Dell knew it, and felt a flash of sorrow that strength such as her mother once knew must in time grow brittle.

"No," The Sir excused her. "We'll need rope, and the axe and the saw, that big Swede saw I think..."

"Sonya, hon, you get the saw. It's on that hook by the back door. Sarah, find the length of rope for your father."

Sonya's hair was half up in curlers. Sarah was in her nightgown and wrapper. Poor female things. Mom could remember at least the strengths that rippled now in Dell's blood, but those two would never know or miss them. Their birthrights had been traded away for back seat kisses and rings. Dell often forgot they were her sisters. They no longer tried to draw her into their snares. Lipstick bait and mirror promises did not tempt her.

Dell helped herself to the strong black coffee, polluted it with cream and two teaspoonfuls of sugar. Nothing was said to her about drinking coffee at midnight. She sensed that somehow this night her place within the family had shifted, that she now filled a niche that had never before existed. It was a strange and heady feeling, like the hot coffee coursing down her throat and uncurling in her stomach. Her face and feet stung. Her thighs burned. They would, she knew, be a lobster red tomorrow. She would have to wear tights to school to cover them.

"Ready?" Her father had the gear, and George was pulling his parka hood up. Dell stomped her boots hastily on, shrugged back into the too-large parka.

They plunged forth once more into the night. For a few moments Dell regretted going into the house at all. She was now aware of the sweat dampness of her socks, of the cold reaching up her back where her coat did not fit tightly, of the swiftly renewed tingling in her face and feet. But there was work to be done, and she would have no one say tomorrow that she was but one of the girls, or too small to help.

George and The Sir busied themselves with the hacking apart of the carcass. She watched as they divided the front legs from the chest, the chest from the hindquarters at the point where the backbone and gut shell narrowed. The pieces were still immensely heavy and unwieldy. She heard them grunt as they sought for purchase to drag them. She moved to help, but The Sir's voice stopped her.

"Dell, we've got this. You load up those guts and the head and get rid of them."

Dell grinned faintly in the darkness. He was telling her her what to do, not how to do it. All right, then.

She moved silently to obey.

The gut pile had frozen into a semi-solid, outwardly leathery heap. The head was heavy, but easy to get a grip on as long as Dell was not too fastidious about blood. She thrust one arm under the stub of throat, and brought that hand up to grip an ear. Hugging the grisly trophy to her, she tottered it over to the wheelbarrow. She dropped it in, and it landed with a smacking noise against the cold metal. It had not landed well. The wheelbarrow would be difficult to balance. But when Dell went to rearrange the load, she found that the head had retained just enough warmth and moisture to bond firmly to the cold metal. The head would not move. One eye glared at her; or was it dark mockery? For the first time that evening she felt a faint unease about the death they had wrought. But no matter. She turned her thoughts from it.

Meat, just meat. No different from hamburger, really.

The gut sack was impossible. There were no grips. There was nothing solid about it. Trying to lift it was like trying to eat soft jello with a fork. Her hands and arms passed through it, to emerge bloodied, but unladen.

She made numerous frustrating attempts. Behind her she could hear George and The Sir hauling off the meat. They must not come back to find her here, to help her. She must not be the last, and with her task undone. She knew what would happen. They would send her into the house, to bed, while they finished the task she was too weak to accomplish. She would be one with the children and helpless women in the house.

In the grip of panic, she seized the great gut pile, unmindful of the blood and slime that coated her chest. She was able to get it half into the wheelbarrow, with half adangle. She scooped it up. Dell could feel a sticky blob of blood or guts on her cold chin. The blood had soaked her mittens, and the wool of them became stiff as cardboard with the freezing gore. But the wheelbarrow was loaded.

Dell moved around, seized the wooden handles, lifted.....and nearly lost her whole load in the snow. She was breathing hard now with effort and frustration. She wiped the hair back from her eyes, coating her cheek and forehead with dampness in the process. But she was no longer considering what she was getting all over herself. She would get the task done.

She lifted the handles again, with as little success. Then, inspired, she turned her back to the wheelbarrow, and seized the handles on either side of her as if they had been the shafts of a wagon and she a dray horse. She pulled, and it budged, but barely. The wheel had frozen solidly in place. Stubbornly she leaned into her task, and the wheelbarrow became a one runnered sleigh behind her.

Clumsily she moved off. She knew exactly what she would do with her load. On the wooded back acre of their lot was a place where, earlier in the summer, she had contemplated building a fort. She had dug a pit there, with no very clear idea of how it was to be incorporated into the fort. Perhaps as an underground cavern? But when she had got chest deep, she had been stopped by permafrost. She had lost interest in the fort plans, then, gone on to other things. But the deep narrow pit had remained. She could dump the crud there, kick loose snow down on top of it. It would be as good a burial place as any.

The load was heavy and the barrow frustratingly unstable. It was all she could do to keep it upright and make any forward progress. Whenever she stopped, she must fling herself around and seize it to keep it from tipping. She could only resume forward motion by sawing the wheelbarrow back and forth in the snow behind her. Soon she forgot about the cold, except for her fingers and toes and face. The rest of her was bathed in the heat of effort. But she did mind the icy air she sucked into her laboring lungs. Her damp scarf across her mouth and nose was more of an annoyance than anything else, and did little to warm the frigid air she breathed.

The path gave out, and she was faced with hauling the wheelbarrow through unbroken snow. It came not quite to her hips. She would have despaired completely, had she not found that at least it solved the problem of the wheelbarrow being tippy. If she could manage to break her own trail and haul it through the snow, it would not now tip over. She redoubled her efforts, leaning into the movement.

Dell was alone in the dark now. The lights of the house were behind her and obscured by a network of trees. Yet her eyes had adjusted to the peculiar half-light that is the darkness of a Fairbanks winter night, and she had no trouble making her way. For was it not her own path that lay beneath her feet, made by her own passage that summer, no matter how obscured now with snow?

At the edge of the pit she stopped and bent over, her damp mittens tucked in between her thighs to suck what warmth they could while she caught her breath. For a moment only she paused thus. There were no sounds to the night, not soughing of wind, not the murmur of far voices. Just silence, and her breathing, and the rush of blood inside her ears.

With various tuggings and mutterings, she maneuvered the wheelbarrow to the edge of the pit. With one final heave born of exultation, she tipped it up. Nothing happened. There was no satisfying slither and plop of evidence into the pit. Dell moved around, peered into wheelbarrow. The guts and head clung to the bottom as if chiseled from the metal itself. The guts must needs be peeled loose of the barrow like a huge scab. The head yielded not to her tugging of its ears, until suddenly one final wrench brought the whole barrow crashing against her and sent the great head tumbling into the pit.

Dell rubbed at her ribs and hip bones where the barrow edge had connected. There would be bruises then, tomorrow, too. She breathed out deeply then, and realized she was trembling, but from cold or exertion she could not tell. She circled the pit, kicking loose snow in on top of the guts. She considered the results, gave one last kick of snow to bury a stubborn ear. Gone.

There were still skummings of blood in the bottom of the wheelbarrow, but Dell guessed it didn't matter much. She dragged the barrow back the same way she had come, making better time going toward the lights with no load. She settled the barrow back against the logs. Dell once more wiped her hair back with a frost slimed mitten. She stood a moment more in the darkness by the side of the house. She could hear a faint murmur from within, but ever predominant was the cold silence of the night pressing in all about her. The frozen stars were close tonight. She turned her eyes up to her favorites, to the Big Dipper and the North Star. They would, she knew, be framed in her bedroom window that night. And framed with them would be the tiny red light of the tower that betokened the airport not far away. The airport.

Dell stood still, searching. She found what was troubling her, and hastened to correct it. To the garage for the snow shovel. She ducked beneath the half opened door. George and The Sir were hoisting the last of the meat up. They paid no attention to her small shadow.

The slaughter place was a darker smear of trampled snow in the garden patch. Dell moved about it with the snow shovel, purifying it. She scooped and scattered the white snow from the edges purposefully. She did not wish to even leave the indentation of a shoveling, the mark of a struggle.

She heard the slamming of the door. Her brother and The Sir had gone in, then. She worked on in the darkness. Her fingers were nearly as stiff as her blood frosted mittens. Soon, soon, she promised her icy feet, her spine that ached from shivering. She heard the door open again, and close. She even heard the sounds of her father as he squeaked through the dry snow in his big boots, but did not turn, but only went on with her task. He stood behind her, and she heard him draw on his pipe.

"What are you doing?"

"The blood on the snow. We're right under the landing pattern for the airport. A small plane might notice the blood on the snow."

"Right." Her father turned and walked away. In moments he was back with a snow shovel. They finished the job together, in silence. Then they walked together back to the garage to return the shovels to their correct places. Immense marionettes of meat hung there now, the ropes and beams still creaking as they adjusted to the great weight. It looked more like meat now, but Dell wondered if she could ever bring herself to eat the dead body of a moose.

"Well, we better get in and get some sleep, Dell. School tomorrow."

Dell made no reply. The Sir knew she had no more desire to go to school tomorrow than she had to bury another moose head that night. But her silence would be her answer. She would go. To not go would be to bring up questions, questions that must be answered with lies. Better no questions than lies.

"Impress on Johnny that he isn't to talk about this to anyone, will you?"

Dell nodded. It was The Sir's way of reminding her that she too must keep silence. He should have known there was no need to remind her.

It took forever for her bed to warm her that night. Her hair was damp where she had sloshed the blood and foulness away. But the smell would not leave her. It clung in her nostrils. It was not a bad smell. It was, after all, only blood. Bruno lay by her bed, his great white muzzle across her bloody boot toes.

The tide of her parents' voices washed to her from their room through the wall.

"....like a duck to water. Out there, covering the blood traces by herself. She's a puzzle to me, Lindy."

"She'll do fine. They're all different, Phil, all the kids. Don't worry about it."

"I suppose....."

Dell wrapped her secrets up in her smile. She slept.

Patricia Frankish
BEFORE THE SEASON OF
BIRDS ON THE WARM WIND

Into the dawn-wind floated a lady
Blessed her bird-skin parka
Little birds her envelope.

Looking to sea through ivory goggles
Sea-ice, no men.

Into the house, making broth
Broth from seal bones
Marrow for men?
Survival rations for dogs
Dog ears and toes tucked
        into their sphere-shapes
Dogs here now, no men.

Look to sea through ivory goggles
Sea-ice, no men.

Time to feed the dogs—bones.
Broth for men.

Into the dawn-wind the lady
Glorious gut-skin parka
Walrus gut her cushion.

Looking to sea through ivory goggles
Sea-ice, no men.

Woman-self and her child eat broth
Nothing for dogs
Nothing for men.

Tomorrow we eat a dog—
My mother, my child, me.

And the other morrows
And the morrows with no men.

Today we eat broth.

Tina Parke-Sutherland
LUCY

Lucy, a shaman's daughter,
sits beside me in the classroom
and complains she hasn't eaten good

since leaving Arctic Village. Do I know
where she can get some fish? I don't,
I'm sorry. She thanks me

with a sideways glance and finally
I recognize her face--The Blessed Damosel,
Rossetti's Lady of six-hundred

canvases and poems--and see her
sitting for her husband's friend.
She tips her chin a bit. Her eyelids drop

until the darkened lashes
brush the cheeks.
Her hair, full with the morning light,

streams through the studio
and pools into a vision
of a woman ringed by smoky bands

of arctic sun. She bends above the morning
cooking-fires, hears the jagged grind
of ice against the gravel bank,

and poses for the river,
shares its magic. Her brilliance
breaks the painter's light

into pure color. Her eyes
are prisms, bending through space
the light he tries to reassemble.

She focuses. He burns and paints
one more way
light moves over water.

Linda Schandelmeier
WORDS FOR A GRAND-DAUGHTER

After the fire we came here,
to a bay shining with salmon, and forests
black with spruce.
      We carved our first boat
out of that wood, days and nights of intense labor,
the sun and moon unnoticed in the sky
burned like faroff lamps.

Then the cow's milk dried up, and the garden
curled under from an early frost.
      The children caught in a whirl
of hunger and bad dreams, my husband a shadow
of someone alive. What little money there was
went for drink, the days soured.

The same crows in the morning, fogbound on the
pilings, the ocean shuffled into the slough
      like always, but the children
were sinking like dead stars.

They escaped one by one.
The eldest took the skiff across the bay.
      My letters came back unopened.
The youngest didn't return from fishing. Pieces
of his boat washed up along the shore.

Your mother said I was dead and now she
won't tell where they put me down—
      It doesn't matter.
The earth is already drawn tight across my chest.

Near the old house your reflection
in the slough is vague. The water remembers my face,
confuses yours, the lines
unmistakably the same.

Jean Anderson

SKIN

On the sidewalk outside Co-Op Drug, and in the street, drunks shimmered like mirages. Lucy watched them from Co-Op's entryway, their slow steps twisted by the door glass to a dance that swayed and wavered, ugly, catching the noon heat. The sight made her think, miserably, of her girlhood, these Second Avenue drunks in Fairbanks so like all the ones she remembered from home, from Rampart, drunken Indians. One of those Rampart drunks had been her youngest uncle, and she could still—even after the sliding away of forty-five years—not think of Uncle Ralph without seeing saliva— Or a thick string of drool, maybe— Saliva, which hung always, it seemed in her memory, from Uncle Ralph's lips—

He'd died of drink. At twenty-seven. There at home, dragged in from the riverbank to die quietly in her parents' bed, not of TB as they said in Rampart, but of drink. She had been eleven, her face hidden (for days after, it seemed—) for days (and before—) in the dusty, warm peace of the dog's coat, there on the porch. The old dog, Scout he had been, panting, panting, so warm. And her whole face and body pressed down on the porch floor into deepest dog—

Now she opened one glass door slowly and stepped out, dry heat rising from the cement like old wind. She stopped there where she stood, her white slacks glowing as cloud above the yellow plastic luster of her sandals. And the door's swish and thud behind her was a sound erasing all her careful intent—which had been to stride, purposefully, through these clusters of wavering, shabby men (and some women, too) who were "visiting"— "Visiting," here on the sidewalk in Fairbanks— Drunks. To walk among these drunks without looking to left or to right, until she reached the parking lot and the cool, dark safety of the Lincoln—

Instead she stood still, her heart thumping as she pulled sunglasses from the flowery pouch that was the front of her kuspuk blouse and adjusted the silvery ear hooks. With two fingers (fingers which shook stupidly) she pushed against the nose piece, its sheen of glass stars rough to her fingertips even when she was sure the glasses rode squarely upon the short bridge of her nose, and— yes, all the world was green. She straightened her spine then and stepped forward again, the hot air surging, catching up her face and her body in thickened heat as she left the pale shade of Co-Op's marquee—

Maybe Howard had been right. He had not wanted her to come. She had, Howard said, her reputation to consider. "Watch and see, Lucy," he'd said. "You'll be sorry. You'll dirty those new sandals in sidewalk beer. Or vomit—" And he'd frowned with the face of his own joke, those last words of Howard's still following her when she backed the perfect, ten-year-old Lincoln down the driveway at eleven. Its air conditioner beginning to hum and her eyes seeing only the dishes stacked neatly in the dish strainer, Howard's pipe in his one hand and the striped dish towel draped around his neck in just that way she always told him not—

And she'd driven downtown so slowly, careful, those words humming: "You'll be sorry—" And herself walking so slowly then, half dazed and trying, trying to feel— casual. Walking at first (like practice) through Penney's bright aisles, dazed— Because in Penney's you never saw drunks.

But Co-Op was doing July inventory, had advertised rabbit skins. White and cross rabbits, too, as it turned out. More fine than the newspaper sketch she had smoothed with her fingers on the kitchen table, for Howard. Two thick and beautiful stacks of them, so soft and silky and luxurious, though of course only rabbits— For 69ᶜ each. It was a bargain. She could not remember seeing such a bargin. And Roxanne, her own only grandchild, and Ruth's only daughter, was pregnant for the first time. Only—? As Ruth was Lucy's (and Howard's) own only daughter, only—? Their only child— For Howard had not been— And she herself, no—

But surely Roxanne would produce a female child. Another beauty. The fourth, in generations, she would be— And these rabbit skins would become a new baby bunting for her. Booties, too, yes— Beautiful and white, with those soft, soft red-brown spots like patches of time caught up— And— Beautiful.

Lucy pulled the crackly pinkness of the plastic Co-Op sack (filled up with the sixteen cross-rabbit skins) tight against her breasts and began to step off the curb. Second Avenue was a smell like beer and sweat, the hot breath of cars— And noise that swelled in your ears— But those rabbit skins had all been gentle and clean, pure to your fingers, there in Co-Op, and she would begin the bunting today. This afternoon—
Because skin sewing was something you could love safely. An Indian thing, for she remembered her aunts and her grandmother and sometimes even Mama, too, sewing skins, in Rampart. And Howard could tease her about it, though he rarely did anymore. Because people were beginning to call her ''an Athabaskan artist'' now. A skin sewer. ''Preserving a traditional art form'' was what that last woman, from the Arts Association, had said at the school, in May—
But once, that one time only, Howard calling her ''my skinny squaw''— That time when Roxanne (a little girl then) had braided the long neckcurls— (Herself Roxanne's own ''Mem-mem'' then—) Roxanne braiding Mem-mem's ''little Orphan Annie perm,'' which was what Howard still always called this hairstyle— (Because he'd chosen it: ''One of the first ones in Fairbanks, too, Lucy!'' His face proud, beaming—) Those neckcurls twisted into a single short cluster of braid: ''My skinny squaw—''
But Howard had always been more a father. Twelve years older— She, always, ''the baby,'' the prettiest and youngest, at home, too, back in Rampart. And—
And it was no lie to live now in their own suburban house. A clean and beautiful home. Her neatly-boxed skins all kept in the pantry beside the dishwasher. No lie to love— Because, yes, she did love the skins— Sewing them, touching—

And Howard was an Indian, too, of course.
And she felt only sometimes that small twinge of something (like shame it seemed, though that was ridiculous—) when she and Howard went (as they so often did now) to address the grade school children in Fairbanks, telling those children— Telling them, now that Howard had sold his optical shop and retired completely (two years ago, that was)— Telling all those sweet gardens of child faces what it was to be an Indian— (The soles of the yellow sandals sticking— In beer, maybe—? Not—? But almost across now, to the parking lot, yes, there soon—)
And, yes, you could love skin sewing—
''The skins were always clean, that's what I remember,'' she'd said

last May, her mind—and her soul, too—pulling away from her so
strangely there, as she stood on that cool, foreign little stage— (For the
stages, in the gyms they were always, never really—) There, during that
most recent grade school visit. In May, it was— And Howard staring so
strangely across the stage into her face, shaking his head slightly, frown-
ing that small, small frown—

"The skins were always clean—" Her own voice. "The fur was
warmer that way, warm and clean. And the Indian people, back home,
the old people, they shook them carefully. Before and after using them,
they shook them to keep them clean. And there was a fine, pure scent,
too—" Shaking her own head— "I don't know— They cared for them,
though, it's true. Hung them from moose or caribou horns on the walls
of the cabins inside, yes, sometimes. And they were beautiful. So
beautiful— Some made into parkas and hats and the small baby
things— Or blankets, small baby blankets crocheted from strips of rab-
bit skin— So soft and always clean— Always—" Howard's small
frown—

Oh, it frightened you, to feel your own mind dance away from you
like that, carrying something—your soul or your spirit— Carrying your
whole self dancing away into some past that seemed almost a future,
and seemed right— Yes, right.

And now someone was saying, a voice behind her saying: "Lucy.
Goddamn, Lucy, that's you. Lucy—"

And she was turning to meet the voice. And yes, yes— No.

It was George. For thirty-five years, maybe, she had not seen him
once. George. And he still stood like a skinny boy there, slim and wiry
as any boy, but balder, a little— His body wavering before her eyes.
George.

And he was hugging her then and the rabbit skins, hugging— That
plastic sack crackling between them there, in the street in front of—
While cars moved around them and someone laughed—

"Oh, George," she said, her own voice saying it— "George,
George—"

"Goddamn if it isn't you," he said. "Goddamn if it isn't you,
Lucy." No drool from his lips and he smelled only of cigarettes, but his
body still— Yes. It wavered away from her and then close again— And
tears, yes, tears. She was weeping against his chest. Cigarette smoke—

"Don't cry, Lucy," George said. "Come have a beer." And he was
holding the sack, the pink crackly sack of rabbit skins under his right
arm, pushed way up under his armpit, her shoulders held tight with his
left arm— Weeping, she— He taking the sunglasses from her face and
leading her across the street and in— Yes— Into the worst bar of them
all. The worst Native bar where Lucy had never, ever been before—

"You look—" she said, weeping—

"Firefighting," George said. "I've been firefighting. At Nenana—" And he was grinning, hugging her again, his body smoky but with cigarettes only— And she— Yes, crying, crying— Hugging—

"Thirty-five years," George said. "Thirty-five. Yes, Lucy, it's you." And he was hugging her again.

"Oh, George—" Crying. The pink plastic crackling against— Crying—

"Two beers," George said. "Two," holding up two fingers toward the back of— and people were looking— A laugh— And a chair, yes, a chair— George was fitting her body to that dirty-looking chair. And crying, she—

"A beer," George said, pushing the glass into her fingers. "You look fine," he said, "not like an old lady, Lucy—"

"And you—" Crying, she— "George— Oh, George—"

"Well, we should have," he said, putting his own glass on the table with both hands. "When we were eighteen in Rampart, Lucy, we should have got married and be damned if—"

And her whole life— No, no. He could not take her whole life from her like that. Catch up her whole life and take it back. No. "Oh, George," she said, "but we—"

"I know," he said. "I know, Lucy. I was too damned rough for you." And he was crying too, almost, then laughing— A drunk's laugh. Uncle— Then grinning, grinning holding her right hand— The pink sack on his knees now— Grinning. "Not an old man, yet, huh? Firefighting," he said, thumping his chest. "In Nenana." Grinning—

Crying, she— "At fifty-six? Firefighting, George?" He, too, fifty-six— Firefighting. "Oh, George," she said. "You—"

"No, no," he said. "We Lucy. We. We still have it." Then: "Drink your beer, Lucy." And he, curling her fingers around the cold wet— With his fingers—

"I don't want any beer, George—" Her glass on the table. There. And the skins, yes— Back on her lap, yes. Safe. The plastic crackle— He patting her both hands— Holding them, holding— "George, I—"

"Yes," he said. "Yes, Lucy, we still—"

"No," she said. "No, George, I've got to—"

Grinning, grinning— "Yes—"

"I'm married, George, and my life has been—"

"Yes," he said. "I know. I can see that, Lucy." That laugh again, then grinning, grinning, holding her both hands. "I can see—" Then, suddenly: "By Christ, you're a white woman, Lucy!" Like a shaman speaking, in him, George— But no shaman, George. Him laughing again, that laugh like a cough— Uncle—

"No, George, I—" But that laugh again—

"Yes, Lucy, a white woman! And still my Lucy," more softly now, patting her both hands with his. "Still prissy—" And that laugh— "You're a prissy white woman now, Lucy."

And: "George!" She, yes— That slap. The sound. Her own fingers tingling, and— Even in the darkness, the beery half light of that awful bar— Yes, red. Her own hand's mark there bright against his cheek. Red, red, her own hand's mark—

All the way to the parking lot, through her tears, Lucy could still see it. Even when she leaned, hot, with both hands and her forehead pressed against the searing white metal of the Lincoln's perfect paint. That ache in her throat now and sobbing. Yes— She could still see that spot bright against his cheek like a scrap of red fox skin.

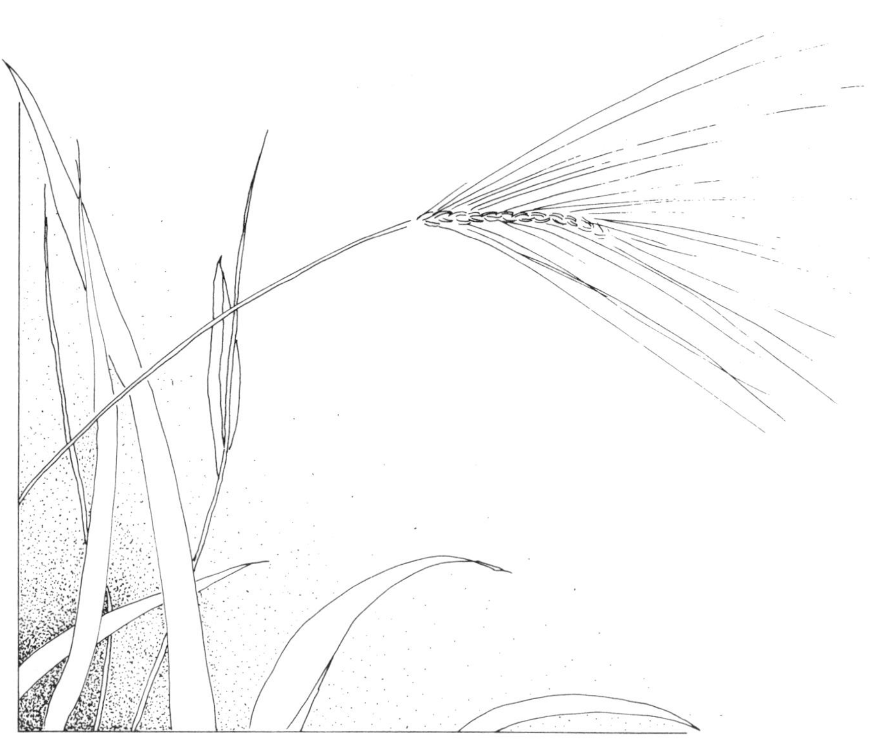

Patricia Monaghan
WE ARE THE VILLAGE

       I leave you in the
night and go to friends. How can
a white man, new to us, know
about me what they know? I need
no excuses. I drink strong coffee
with my beer. They know me.

       You lie balled
in a sleeping bag beside your stove,
your sad sleek body distant, slender
as the moon. I sit six houses away
weeping over you, furious because
you have a questing mouth, because
you could leave for good, for nothing.

       I go to the bar from
here. I do not need you to buy me beer.
My friends are there. They will let me
cry and rage: at your slow eyes that pretend
to know us, slow fingers that stroke me
like porcelain or some rare animal, rage
at all your mockery, your hungers, the black

       hairs curling on your belly.

Katherine McNamara
THE VISITOR

One day a man, his wife, their friend,
and a visitor drank whiskey
and set out down river in a boat.

There was an accident, the man fell overboard.
His friend, the driver, drove blind drunk.
The man got cut by the propeller.
His wife barely managed to pull him into the
                    boat.
Somehow they got home.
Later, she alone remembered the visitor
who had fallen in at the same time.
Men dragged the river.
No luck.

If the driver was drunk,
and if the wife chose—terrible choice,
having had to choose—to save
her husband first, then who could have saved
the visitor?

As for the wife, she remembers
only one moment of this drowned man:
in the corner of her eye he is falling
and then he is out of her sight.
Not even that God turned His back
on this visitor,
but that he slipped
through the net of kinship and drowned
because no one could attend to him.

Patricia Monaghan
BUSH PILOT'S WIFE

Flailing like an insect—
a wind-smashed moth
against the tinted glass—
he died at eighty knots
and ten thousand feet.
His heart gave out.

All I knew of flying then
was how to land. Was it enough?
Below us, braided rivers
twisted like collapsing veins
and a dead-blue glacier
stretched out like a corpse
or like a runway.

I leaned across
his flapping body—
my moth-husband,
oh my firefly—
and only later tried
to revive him with
that parody of kisses.
I brought us down. I
could not bring him back.

What I know of flying now
is everything I need,
a cocoon of loneliness
around a secret strength:
the knowledge that just once
the frailest butterfly
survives its own emergence.

Nancy McCleery
THE VOICE OF HORSE

The horse, slow to go up the mountain,
was no wild horse needing to be broken,
only like its bastard brother mule
who moves decisively; so that the woman
who rode the horse only once at eighteen
and heard he had thrown Reeva her friend
only the year before, breaking her ankle
and her spirit up into limpings and stumblings,
after only once, is the woman who runs
from horse, doesn't like the feel of him
against her thighs, is afraid he will step
on her feet as she mounts. She hears
in his every neigh the voice of a stallion
who bites a mare at the neck to break
her in.

Cynthia Hardy
NATURAL FORCES

She was flying high into the arms of the firs, sighting down her legs to them on the upswing, curving toward them on the hard seat as she swung back down. As she reached the height of each backswing she lifted herself off the seat a little, then slammed down, forcing herself back through the arc till she could see the tops of the trees again, just out of reach of her bare toes. Sometimes she would tip her head back and glide, watching the ground dip and rise beneath her. Once, as she lifted her head to pump against the ropes, she saw a man sitting on the park bench across the path, watching her. She leaned back her head for one more glide, then raised it again on the next swing. He had a hand in one pocket of his jacket; the other hand held a cigarette off to the side, the smoke curling aimlessly over the park grass.

At the next swing she noticed the darkness about his eyes. It seemed to her a thoughtful intensity. She glanced at him over the top bar when she reached the peak and swung back down. Perhaps he knew what would happen if ever once she swung well enough and hard enough to actually close the gap between the trees and her toes. She arched her body back against the air, pointing her toes in a clean curve toward their goal. The clouds, which had been a pale even gray above her began to gather into a knot and darken. As if their collecting shadow

39

was a signal, she stiffened her legs and let them drag in the dust again and again.

When she looked again, the man had gone. The air seemed moist as though the cloud were breathing chilly down on her. She rubbed her arms and headed down the wide park walkway. During the long summer days in this city, the weather changed abruptly, drawing her moods along with it. At first she had not noticed the connection and thought herself depressed. Now she accepted these shifts in weather and mood believing she had allied her rhythms with the forces of nature. On days like this one, she watched pigeons wheel above the roof tops and from time to time found herself taking a man back with her to her room.

The clouds were clotting in places and thinning in others. In a bright patch further down the park she saw the man again, sitting facing her approach. She hesitated. He *was* looking at her. Her stomach began to roll as it did in moments of choice. She could take what was offered or resist, and with an empty Saturday afternoon spread before her, she chose.

The man grinned at her, pulling thin lips back from uneven teeth. "Do y'know the time?" he asked. She took a step closer and he stood to meet her. "Watch stopped." He twisted his wrist in rapid flicks as if to prove the truth of his statement.

"Oh," she said. Her stomach had stopped rolling and she gave herself over to the moment, deeply calm, as she had learned to do when travelling north on the jet, when she had told herself at each takeoff, "OK, now, whatever comes." He edged nearer.

"You see, I have to catch a plane at four," he said. She started. Telepathy. A gift of fate. "There's a clock on the bank on Fifth Street," she said. "It must be about two."

Something was working behind his smile. She wondered what to do next. "I could show you where the clock is," she offered. It wasn't exactly right, but it seemed to encourage him. "I saw you swinging up there," he said. She laughed, uncertain. He took a few steps down the path. "I wonder if you could help me." She matched his steps. "I dunno. How?"

He seemed to measure her for an instant. "You look, y'know, like you might help somebody out. I just got out of jail. I don't know anybody here." A muscle at the back of her neck twitched at the words, but her calm persisted. If nothing else, she made a point of listening to any story. He studied her hesitation.

"Hey, it's nothing serious. Busted on a marijuana charge. Me and my girlfriend. She's still down in California. Coming back next week." He reached out and took her wrist, his grip firm, alive, and she felt a little thrill of warmth run up her arm.

"You have small hands. Good." She had always thought them large

— an awkward part of her stuck on the end of wrists that stretched too far out the ends of her sleeves. "Here's how you can help me. My girlfriend stashed some dope in a crack in an old pipe up the hill there." He pointed to an area where the park sloped up to the forest preserve. "Her hand just fit into the pipe, but mine's too big. Yours would fit."

She shook her head doubtfully. They had left the path and began to cross a wide grassy area leading down to the track. Three runners in jogging suits of blue, red, and orange paced loose-jointedly around the far curve. "My hands are no smaller than yours," she said. Something in all this eluded her. The delicacy of his tone, the slight wounded pout of his mouth, runnels of feeling barely concealed beneath the restless gestures.

He stretched out his hands to match hers, then stiffened and stretched his fingers so that they extended slightly beyond hers. "See," he said. In an infinite universe anything is possible, she thought. Her hands could be small. "Ok. I'll do it."

The clouds had thinned and split all across the sky and the grass seemed mottled, shifting as the shadows slid over it. The vastness of the field opened around her and she moved closer to the man as if he could steady her from falling into the grassy depths.

He began to talk rapidly about himself — his time in jail, the girl in California, fierce as a lynx, the boat he would buy with the money from a dope deal, the long trip island-to-island to Singapore. There was an inventiveness in his words that charmed her and lulled her. For a while, she heard only the tone of his voice, rolling, beguiling, and saw only the rapid, starling movements of his eyes, the flutter of his hands.

They approached the woods at the far end of the park. He became increasingly agitated and she reached out her hand to him. He jumped at her touch. "I keep looking for cops," he said. He was looking everywhere but at her. "That was a long time ago," she said. He looked straight at her then and again her stomach rolled.

"I'll give you some money," he said. She shook her head and a strand of hair clung across her throat. "No, it's OK." He studied her for a moment, then took her hand which still lingered in the air between them and tugged at it. "Come on."

The path under the trees, littered with needles, muted their steps as they walked. He had her hand firmly now, pulling against it with each step up the hill. Looking back she could see the open park, joggers bobbing, couples strolling. The woods seemed remote from the lawns they had just left as if a wall of shadow, of silence, had descended when they entered. They did not speak. From moment to moment she forgot why they had come and concentrated only on stepping silently, smoothly over the needles and twigs. The dimmed light seemed to come from all directions at once so that objects seemed equally illuminated, equally shadowed. An amanita glowed at a bend in the path ahead of them, but when they reached it he turned abruptly toward her, kicking it with a careless motion of his foot.

"It's around here somewhere." His fingers pressed tight against the bone of her hand. She stared down at the creamy flesh of the mushroom where the red skin had split and thought of a book, opened pages down. They had stopped and he was peering into the woods off the path, then back at the green space below and behind them. Suddenly he pulled her into a small flat open spot behind a large fir.

"Get down. I see somebody coming." There was no one that she could see, but he pulled down sharply on her hand so that she folded slowly to the ground. They sat silently there for a few seconds, peering out between the trees, watching for anyone who might come along the path. She began to wish they were done with this errand. Once his patter of words had ended she found her calm eroded by a spreading numbness. She glanced down at her hand, still tight in the grip of his, then looked across at him.

He was looking at her. A muscle jumped in his cheek, but his eyes were steady on hers, insistent.

"Where's the pipe?" she asked. Her voice sounded high and flat in her ears. She couldn't remember when she had last spoken. He held a finger to his lips, glanced back at the path, then whispered again sharply, "Stay down." With his free hand he pushed her head toward his chest and curved across her so that her cheek pressed the wales of his corduroy jacket and she could see nothing but ferns tangled against each other at the roots of the fir.

His hand began to move slowly over her hair, then traced small circles at the nape of her neck. She could hear a slight wheeze in his chest as he breathed and the rapid, distant thumping of his heart. So this was it — the heartbeat, the breath, the moving hands.

"You must be lonely," she said. She reached her arm around his chest, patting the corduroy gently. "Yeah," he said, "It's lonely in prison." She sensed a lie, but ignored it for he had let go her hand and pressed his lips against her mouth, pushing her down with his other hand. He held her tightly, as if expecting her to resist, but she pulled him against her, allowing a familiar warmth to spread in her. She felt a twig pressing jaggedly against her back as his hands moved down, saw the light shift like pale coins through the branches above her. She loosened his belt, his fly and pushed the cloth away from his body, then tugged her own jeans down and arched against him.

It was over quickly. Then she lay stretched on the bristling ground, listening to his breathing as it slowed, her arms absently draped across his back. She felt an ache drumming in her chest, so large and empty it seemed about to swallow her from within. His head pressed against her cheek; he was whispering something she couldn't quite hear. She pushed against him and rolled away to pull the denim back up over the pale brightness of her skin.

He rose up on one elbow. His eyes seemed bluer, clearer now, but she didn't care. "You're really something," he said. She shrugged. He fumbled with his clothes, watching her. She waited, thinking of her room, her chair, her things. "That was all a lie about the dope in the pipe, you know," he said. She looked out over the ferns at a shard of green lawn. "I know," she said.

He felt in his pocket for something. "Look," he said. As she turned toward him he clicked open a thin sharp blade. He turned it in his hand; it sliced the dimness as it moved.

"Look. Here's what I was going to do. I was going to get you to come with me with that story about the dope. Get you greedy by offering you money. Then when I found the right spot I'd take this," he waved the knife at her. She sat stone still. "And hold it here," he drew a finger across her throat. "And then I could do what I wanted with you. I worked it all out watching you on that swing." She remembered him sitting there, watching her, one hand in his pocket. He had been fingering that knife.

He flicked the blade back into its sheath.

"But, hell, you were nice to me."

She had stopped listening. She rose slowly and began to back away as if he were a strange dog growling in her path.

"Hey, wait. I don't have to catch a plane. I made that up. C'mon. I'll buy you coffee and we can talk." He got up awkwardly and stood off balance, pleading. His voice held an ache that matched her own, but her feet had found the packed dirt of the path and she was running down through the trees, each step jarring her muscles loose and flinging her toward the empty field below.

Karen Randlev
CAFE AU LAIT WOMAN

She was just a cafe au lait woman,
tall and stringy,
walking splayfooted down Two Street,
a paper bag fisted in each hand.

Forgetting about her,
I sat in the car eating dinner,
canned shrimp, crackers and milk,
watching the drunks and pipeliners,
people in from the village
as they moved on down the street.

But driving away into the night,
I saw her shadow in the doorway
of the Savoy Bar at the corner,
her back to the drunk
she was jerking off
into her paper bags.

*Gisakk — The Russians said they were Cossacks;
some Alaskan Natives now use this term for all
white people.*

Mary TallMountain
SHE'S A HAWK!

But she's a hawk! Tatiana said,
    roundbutton eyes flared.
    I heard her grumble,
    How come *Gisakk* so dumb?

The youngman picked it up.
    The body was a little fist,
    head revolved with a fierce
    yellow stare.
    It's an owl, he said.

Gisakk! What's matter you?
    Already he full grown.
    I tell you it mouse hawk.
    She's a hawk!

Grabbing the bird
    She hurried along the boardwalk.
    Shook her head
    Frowned all the way
    out of sight.

Sheila Nickerson
WHITE LILACS

The bitter widow
Down the street
Grows white lilacs,
Or, white lilacs
Have come to bloom
Before her door.
I want her to open
That door with a crash,
Rush down the steps,
Embrace those lilacs like friends
Long gone on a journey,
Hug them and cry
And dance in the yard
And sing to the neighbors
That everything beautiful
Comes again and again,
That no one can be lonely
Who does not choose to be;
And everyone will dance
Until the lilacs burst
Into summer, and only
When we are tired
Will we stop to take
A rest in a quiet time
Called winter.

Ann Chandonnet
CURLED MINT
(for Nancy)

"Crying," I hear men say,
is "for little girls."
(They particularly say this
to little boys.)
"You do it on purpose,"
they say;
and, on the other hand,
"You lack control."

Big girl,
with my wet badge of courage,
I say,
if liberation is speaking my mind everywhere,
blunt but constructive,
then so is crying.

Especially when another person,
after you have drunk wine
and stood in the barbecue's smoke
sufficiently to demonstrate commitment,
says, "I had a miscarriage four years ago;
I felt useless."
Tears come and brim over
before thought can brim in words.

It is an act of sympathy,
an act of faith,
better than words.
Please understand.

I plant these seeds of Curled Mint.
They do not smell of mint;
they are not green;
I can scarcely feel them between thumb and
                finger,
they are so small.
I plant them anyway,
trusting in sun and rain
and the mysterious body of the earth.

I plant them in a permanent position.
I speak my permanent position,
weep it into smoke.

Please understand:
If we speak and weep,
the mint will grow.
We will harvest it,
dry it,
brew it into tea—
which we will share.

And where the winters are severe,
we will mulch.

DREAMS

Sheila Nickerson
AUGUST DAY: PRELUDE

In the sky,
          an unrest of crows;
in the trees,
          the ashberries gone red.
In the first falling leaves,
          a woman holds
sheet music in her arms.

Katherine McNamara
THE BERRY PICKERS

Down, down
        to the bogs
they drift
        with nestling down
        of fireweed topping;
through currents of seeds,
        bird-fields, down
        fine and white as hair,
white and gray as clouds
in a milky sky

the women come
        to the bogs,
buckets slung on sturdy,
        slender arms.

        It turns late
in the season for berries,
        threatens rain.
Their probing fingers glean

the soggy muskeg, scratched,
stained with juice, blood.
Stooping, plucking,
        tasting,
        pails slowly filling,
they slosh,
        small domestic figures,
from mound to dense mound.

            plock plock
        Flat off red hills,
        hunters' echoes.
        Gathering's slow,

surer. Gatherers,
gleaners now so late into summer,
play this game for pies.
                    Their paths
uncurl from the center
of each small territory;
they are spread like nets
        across fields.
They bend nearer earth cradled in hills,
        heedless as feasting bears
        rambling all fall
toward their juiced and sugared
        denning.

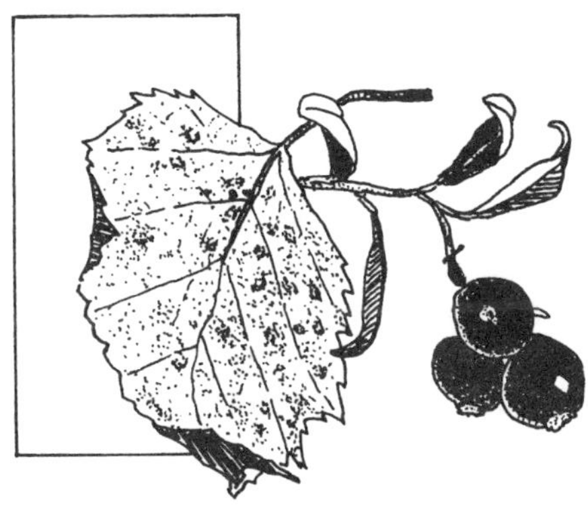

Karen L. Kohout
BLUEBERRY PICKING IN ALASKA

He rolled onto Nicole's side of the mattress and propped his head on her pillow. A beam of light poured through the opposite wall. He considered the window, a six-paned horizontal rectangle, its wood surfaces layered with green paint. Military surplus, he surmised. Which of Nicole's past partners had procured and installed it? Or had it been acquired by one and fashioned into the log wall by another?

No matter. The sun shone and they would pick blueberries today. Nicole would be in a good mood: talkative, receptive. She would learn he intended to join that procession of Nicolean helpmates into retirement. What memorial would he leave to his three month's residence? He'd procured no window; installed nothing unless you counted a few repairs. He'd send her something from Mexico or Australia. For now, she'd have to settle for a bucket of blueberries.

He smiled, envisioning his name encircled by a flashlight beam on one of several plastic pails lined up on a shelf in the dank cellar beneath the cabin. Shivering, he pulled the quilt up under his chin, the stiff curls of his beard brushing the backs of his hands. The beard, his first, would be all he'd take from this place that he hadn't brought. He hadn't so much as a chapter outline of his novel. Still cold, he turned his thoughts back to the sun and the prospect of fair weather after two weeks of scud.

They would go blueberry picking as soon as the weather changed, she'd said. It was the end of August, too late in the season to count on it not freezing at night once the cloud cover moved on. If it frosted, the fruit would soften, dusky skins wrinkling, pulling away between one's fingers from bleeding purple flesh. They'd not keep fresh then and she'd have to preserve them, leaving none whole for pancakes or just eating with sugar and milk. He struggled with a vision of Nicole aproned amongst gleaming jars and steaming kettles.

Ingenuous caprice was a quality she shared with this life, this environment that simply existed from one day to the next with no apparent regard for past or future short of adhering to a rough outline of seasonal change. It was the intermittent conformity to universal order that disarmed.

Foraging inspired the poet in Nicole, her green eyes warming as she extolled the painful pleasures of stalking the *Vaccinium caespitosum*. One groped for footing among tussocks that thrust deceptively solid-looking grass heads up from the tundra floor. The prospect of twisting an ankle as one slipped off a niggerhead into six inches of cold black muck tied knots in one's nerves. Ah, but on a sunny day with the leaves of the berry bushes splashed red against the yellow grass, dwarfed by jeweled birch saplings and the bare corpses of black spruce still standing a decade after a fire. . . It aroused him as he lay warming under Nicole's comforter to recall her description of finding a dry place where one could sit or lie curled among sun-warmed niggerheads to pluck ripe fruit from all the branches within a body's reach. He was imagining her small form under him, her pale skin streaked blue, the scent of bruised labrador tea. . . when a knocking on the floorboards shook him from his reverie.

A bird-knuckled hand rapped the floor near the hole that accommodated the ladder between the loft and main room of the cabin and was joined by the other, clutching a steaming mug; then, the white center part of her dark hair, slender high forehead, large eyes, longish nose, fragile mouth, and pointed chin as she ascended. "Coffee time," she asserted in the frail voice that, nonetheless, seemed always to convey finality to the most mundane comment.

"Great day for blueberry picking," she said. Her eyes widened meaningfully, then receded, followed by her head and hands down the ladder, leaving the mug at the edge of the hole. He crawled, shivering again, from under the cover to fetch and bring the mug back to the floor at the side of the mattress. He settled back, pulling the quilt up over his chest, leaving his arms and shoulders exposed so as to be able to cradle the hot mug in his hands.

So, he thought, pleased at having anticipated her, they would pick blueberries today. They would not, of course, make love among the niggerheads and labrador tea. Anything less than full protection against tne assaults of mosquitoes and no-see-ums on the tundra was unthinkable, not to mention the embarrassing prospect of being mistaken for a blueberry bush by a nearsighted bear. But it would be a congenial time to tell her it was time for him to move on.

He'd met her in Fairbanks in late May. "Last-call-want-another?" she'd whispered in that squeaky voice. He'd nursed the same beer for the past hour, uneasily aware of the five a.m. closing time.

"I'm fine," he insisted. He smiled, looking past her, and wrapped large square hands protectively around his quarter full glass. He guessed she'd been waiting this section of tables off and on all night in between sets on the stage. He'd only noticed her at all on stage for her lack of the voluptuousness one expected in a go-go dancer. In another business, she'd be the boss' daughter. Personally, he wouldn't admit owning this joint to his daughter, much less let her work here. His shiny-faced Minnesota prudery seemed out of place, even to himself. Still, he'd just as soon have had somewhere else to go.

She returned minutes later, poured part of a cold beer into a clean glass in front of him and a Seven-up into a second glass across the small table. Dragging a chair from another table, sitting opposite him, she said, "It's on me." He leaned forward to hear her. "My last night. I'm off now. Let's celebrate." She reached a small hand over the table and patted his arm. Her bird-boned features were partially obscured in the flashing lights, but he found her attractive in an exotic, un-midwestern way. Two dark streams of hair fell alongside her face, draping her bare shoulders to brush the top of an unrevealing strapless bodice of shiny fabric.

"I go home today," she squeaked. "You look homeless. Want to come along?" He was thrown off guard, but recovered to consider that he'd left home for the first time in his twenty-three years for what? Adventure? Here, it seemed, adventure beckoned. What the hell? It would not do, of course, to seem too eager.

"Where's home?"

"I live in the bush. You know, log cabin, all that. It's about a hundred twenty miles. I have a charter set up for this afternoon at two. You can't bring much gear. I'll have to bump some freight for you. What are you? About one-seventy-five? I can only take a thousand pounds. I always figure nine-hundred plus me. I have to take my dog, too. He's about fifty."

"A charter?" He interrupted her calculations. "You mean a plane. Can't you drive there?" He'd felt himself swept along as she spoke, but was intimidated now by the prospect of getting someplace from where he couldn't just walk away.

"Oh no." She smiled for the first time. "I told you, it's in the bush. There's no road within, oh, there's a village with a road about forty miles away, but it's north of the Yukon. The road doesn't go anywhere."

He'd learned nothing more about her then. Yet, as they walked out of the darkened lounge into the bright morning, he was telling her about himself, feeling she should know what *she* was getting into.

"I graduated last month; took five years, but it got my folks off my back. Dad's a minister; doesn't have a church, though. He's an administrator for an insurance company for ministers. Mom's a nurse, or was. They're very uptight about education; had me programmed for pre-med. Psychology or teaching were Dad's bottom line. He had all he could do to keep his mouth shut when I decided on English. They were so glad to see me graduate, they gave me the money to get to Alaska for a graduation gift. I'm supposed to get the wanderlust out of my system or something.

"There was this guy, Brian: big, dark, a poet. Maybe you've run into him? He'd hang around go-go places." Nicole appeared to consider and shook her head, no. "Brian dropped out of the writing program at U of M last year; was coming up here to get a job on the pipeline. I got a letter from him last winter that said he was waiting to get out as a teamster or laborer. He must have, 'cause I haven't found him."

"So, now you're out of money," she said. "Where're you staying?"

He'd avoided saying that he'd planned to call home that day for money. He'd guessed he'd just go south, California, work his way down to Mexico, someplace cheaper to live. "Out at the Fairgrounds," he answered. "I've got my tent and bag. I move it every few days, try to get next to a family in a camper so I can ask them to keep an eye on my stuff when I'm gone."

"You can stash your tent and gear at a friend of mine's here in town. You won't need it at the cabin. Just bring clothes and personal stuff."

"You don't have a typewriter out there do you? It sounds like a great place to work on my book." He thought of asking her for a small loan to buy some paper, but didn't.

"No, I have paper and pens, though. You're welcome to them if you don't mind writing your book in longhand." She was as matter of fact about his writing as about his being out of money, job and home. "Here's where I stay." They'd turned off Second Avenue at Cushman, turned again at First toward the power plant, and stopped in front of a sagging two-story log house. "My friends are probably still asleep. You can be back here by noon or so with your gear. I have to run some errands, but I'll tell Buck and Jean to expect you. They'll run us out to the air service after lunch."

That afternoon he'd called home, collect, from Buck and Jean's, just to let his parents know he'd be out of touch for a while, "working on my novel. Got a chance to stay at a cabin in the bush, you know, the boondocks, no communications. . ."

He should have asked them to send money. It'd be waiting for him now in Fairbanks, once he figured out how he was getting back to Fairbanks. People had happened by over the summer in float planes or by canoe. Hunting season was coming up and there'd be hunters flying in. Nicole would know the best way. The first step was to break it to her that he'd be leaving, the next chance he got.

He finished the coffee, hustled out of bed into his clothes and down the ladder. Nicole was mounting specimens for her collection — butterflies, thank God. He couldn't abide the impaling of bugs and beetles before breakfast.

"Looks like we have our change in the weather," he said, pulling a stump out from under the table to sit opposite her. She gently adjusted the final pin in a swallow-tail's wing and looked up, an almost-smile playing on her lips, her eyes blinking as though adjusting to a change in light. Her eyes always looked to him as though she should wear glasses. Frames would move them out, away from her nose.

"More coffee?" she murmured as she cleared pins, jars, small white cardboard squares from the table.

"Oh, yeah, I'll get it." He reached for the plaid Thermos bottle on the cold wood stove. "How 'bout you?"

"Hmm?" She was looking at him, calmly, expecting nothing. "Oh, no thanks. I have coffee nerves already. Shall I start some pancakes? Tomorrow we'll have sourdough-blueberry pancakes." She got up and pumped the Coleman stove she used when she didn't want to heat up the cabin or wanted to cook something quick. "We should get moving, take advantage of the weather."

By noon, they'd packed a lunch, three plastic ice cream pails, insect repellant, a water jug, her rifle, and extra cartridges, just in case. They were about to step out of the cabin when Scratch barked from behind the cabin.

They exchanged one brief questioning look before Nicole thrust her rifle, a Marlin .45/70 lever action with several inches cut off the stock and a two inch rubber recoil pad, into his hands and squeaked, "Bear! Go on out. I'll get the camera!"

He thought to hold the screen door, allowing it to close quietly behind him before starting around the corner of the cabin toward Scratch's angry noise. Around the barrel of the ridiculously light rifle he saw the black and white husky pacing along a stretch of trail that passed beneath a large spruce a few yards behind the cabin. The dog's steady gaze, despite its excited perambulations, directed him up the tree. Fif-

teen feet above the ground, a black bear clutched the trunk with all
fours, its head moving back and forth in rhythm with the dog's pacing.

"Thataboy, keep it up there, Scratch," Nicole's voice encouraged as
she passed behind him with the camera. She stepped in front of him to
get the shot.

"Hey, you're making me nervous," he said. "Is this toy loaded?"

"Sure." She stepped back alongside him. "But there's no shell in the
chamber unless you put one there. Aren't guns always loaded?" She
looked meaningfully up at him. "Let's get this dumb bunny out of here.
We'll have to let it get a good head start before we go now." She called
Scratch who came reluctantly and allowed himself to be held by the col-
lar, sitting at her side. "O.K. Get out of here!" she commanded the
bear. It looked at them, then stretched its neck to peer longingly over its
shoulder down the trail along which it must have approached earlier.
"Yell at it," Nicole hissed, patting his arm.

"Get outa here! Go on! Get!" he threatened. Down came the bear,
paw by paw, dropping the last few feet to all fours on the trail where it
turned a bobbing black bottom to them and fled.

"Go get it, Scratch!" Nicole squeaked as she loosed the straining
dog.

"Now what?" he asked, offering her the rifle.
She declined. "You carry that. I'll take the shotgun as a back-up.
Anyway, we'd better give Scratch a chance to run it off and come back.
Let's go in and have another cup of coffee."
Nicole stood on the board-and-cushion couch to reach the double bar-
reled shotgun hung on nails piercing the log wall, loaded it with two
double "0" shells, and stuffed another two shells into the back pocket
of her jeans. She drank coffee as he exclaimed over how docile and
frightened the bear had seemed. He'd expected an encounter with a bear
in the wild to be more threatening. "Oh, I think it can be," she said
with quiet finality. He went out to see if Scratch had returned.

"I can hear him barking, probably this side of the gravel bar," he
said as he came in. They unpacked the lunch and ate it before he
checked again.

"Still barking; sounds like the same place. I'll bet it's up another tree.
'Course we didn't have too many bears in Minneapolis, in trees or out,
so I could be wrong."

"No. You're probably right. Shall we go give it another chance?"
They started on down the trail, one he had walked a hundred times or
more that summer. It took on new dimensions now with the probability
of a threatened bear in any tree. He carried the rifle out front in both
hands. She followed with the shotgun, a ludicrous picture with her a
bare foot and a half taller than it was long. Halfway between the cabin

and the gravel bar, they heard a sniff, two snorts, and a groan. They stopped.

"Do bears sound like that?"

"I suppose they could," she whispered. "What else could it be?" They had moved toward Scratch's barking. She called to the dog, but his barking continued. "We'd better stay here, don't you think? I mean, with that brush," she indicated the willow and alder thicket through which they would pass if they continued along the path toward Scratch's position, "there's no telling . . ."

"Right," he agreed. "It could be anywhere in there." They stood close together by a large spruce scanning the brush for a sign. They heard another "sniff, snort, snort, groan" before he allowed his eyes to wander above the tops of the stout willows and alders. "There it is!" He pointed to a cottonwood towering fifty feet above the scrub. Thirty feet up, still below the bulk of the foliage, the bear stood forlornly on a sturdy limb, its right paw draped over a higher bough, its left foreleg wrapped around the trunk. From time to time, it raised its head to snap in frustration at the few yellowing leaves dangling from nearby branches.

It took longer, this time, to pry Scratch from his post at the base of the cottonwood deep within the thicket. Nicole led the dog back up the trail to the cabin, shut him inside, and returned. "Still up there?"

"Hasn't budged," he answered. "What if it doesn't come down before dark?"

"We could use the meat."

"Bear?"

"Why not? This close to fall, it may have enough fat on it, we'd get some lard." As they waited for the bear to take some initiative, they watched six ravens appear and circle the top of the cottonwood. One by one each raven dove close to the bear's head shrieking as though finding this particular bear up a tree were some great in-joke among the local wildlife.

"What happens if we just leave it be?" he asked.

"Fine, but I'm not keeping Scratch penned up with a bear around. I have him to run bears off. If we keep him in, that bear will be in the garden, up in the cache, tearing up everything that looks interesting. I'll have to let Scratch out. He'll keep us awake all night barking. Then we'll come out in the morning and shoot the bear."

He was taken back by the defiance, indeed the emotional level, in her tone. She wants to shoot that bear, he thought. Correction; she wants *me* to shoot that bear. "Let's give it a while longer," he said. "Maybe you'd want to go back up to the cabin for some more coffee. I'll keep an eye on it here."

While she was gone, he cleared the brush away from a leaning deadfall where he was able to steady the rifle and sight in on the bear. The weapon's light weight and short length felt wrong for what he knew was a powerful firearm. He couldn't help feeling he was going up against a bear with a twenty-two. The bear continued to sniff, snort, and groan although it made no move to flee. He had begun to share Nicole's exasperation by the time she returned with the Thermos.

"I guess it's a little late to go berry picking now, huh?"

"Yes," she answered, observing the clear but darkening sky. "It's going to freeze tonight too. If we're going to shoot the bear, we'd probably better do it. It's after five. We'll need some daylight to get the hide off and gut it. Then the meat will be o.k. until morning."

He wished she'd cut the "we" business. It was clear she did not expect to shoot the bear herself. "O.K." he said. He stepped over to the leaning deadfall, steadied the rifle against it, aimed, and fired. For seconds the bear clung coughing to the tree. It had been a perfect lung shot, he was certain, and the recoil convinced him the rifle was no twenty-two; but he imagined a couple of hundred pounds of wild hurt plunging thirty feet into the brush and running . . . where? He fired again. The bear fell, disappearing into the willow and alder below. He felt Nicole's hand on his arm.

"Wait," she said. "I'll get Scratch. Let him go in first, o.k.?"

They followed Scratch into the brush and found the bear quite dead. It sounded corny when Nicole suggested they haul it up the trail to the cabin in the wheel barrow, but it worked better than carrying it tied to and swinging to and fro from a pole. Back at the cabin, Nicole snapped a few pictures of him hitched in front of a wheelbarrow full of bear with Scratch sitting alongside the handles.

"Now what, Bush Lady?" He was high. It had been a good shot, she'd said, the first one, no need to have fired the second; he'd see that when they opened it up.

"We skin it out." The animal lay on its back. She made a small cut in the belly skin with the pointed tip of the large blade of a knife she'd taken from her pocket, then employed what she called a "zipper blade" with a rounded tip to open the skin up the belly without risk of cutting into the thin flesh and puncturing the gut. She made cuts down the forearms and legs, appraised the amount of lard they would get as "better than a June bear, not so good as September."

They began the tedious job of skinning, of separating the thin hide from flesh with the least possible amount of fat adhering to the skin. As they worked, the sun set and he found himself warming his hands against the bear's flesh. He thought better of bringing up his plans to leave at the moment and so they worked in silence for a long while.

"Yes," she said as she stopped to warm her hands between her knees, ''we'll get a hard frost tonight. Tomorrow, after we've taken care of the meat, we can go cranberry picking, lowbush cranberries. They ripen with a frost, *vaccinium vitis*. The place where I pick them is like an enchanted forest — ruby red berries dripping from tiny stems that grow up from a moss carpet with stiff white caribou lichen all around. . .''

Cheryl Morse
FISHWIFE

I'm a casual friend of dangerous Edna
All her stories come tumbling out
I find myself pinned to the room
Her fishknife wields in the light
As her men lead her along

The fish at the cannery
With her red scarf and black boots
Give up their spirit to her
She carves them with skill
They become pieces of the sun

Karen Randlev
AT THE KOTLIK CO-OP STORE

The two nuns in Kotlik
wear rubber boots
and green slickers
from Greenland.
Sister Mary Ann eyes the instant oatmeal,
glancing heavenward
before she picks it off the shelf,
the stamp of its $3.59 price glaring at her.

Sister Margaret, on the other hand,
glides down the aisle,
her rubber trousers flapping against her ankles.

She turns only to talk
to old ladies and children,
ignoring a curly-headed
Irish construction worker
buying chew and light bulbs.

I'd like to cross myself,
or genuflect, gain
absolution, give confession
or something parochial,
but my only catholic gesture
is a nervous smile as I back
out the door into the rain.

Karen Randlev
BEARDED LADY IN FAIRBANKS

The first time I saw the bearded lady
was in the Borealis Book Store—
she was complaining to a friend
what a rip-off Welfare was.

I was looking at cookbooks,
but moved over to the occult section
just to get a better look
and to listen to her voice.
How I wanted to reach out
and touch
her curly little patch.

She wore old bib overalls
and a gingham shirt with puffed sleeves.
About 5'4". She must've weighed about 200.
She had bits of yarn wound around
her curly pony tails which matched
the color of her beard.

I really wanted to stroke it.

She chuckled when she bought a book
about sourdough cooking and paid for it
out of a little leather pouch
slung over her hips.

The last time I saw her
she was a driving a '72 Datsun pickup
with a load of hay in the back.
She had her skirt pulled high,
her right leg propped on the dash
as she waited for the light
at University and Airport Road.

I think about her a lot
and wonder whether she has boyfriends,
or a dog, or a cabin in the woods,
but mostly whether she would let me
feel her little frizz of a beard.

Jean Anderson
A MARRIAGE: In medias res
(for Betty)

The dogs came first: six of them, tiny
Alaskans. Then four. (Two killed by larger
dogs—) All strays or from The
Shelter. And then the babies (both
boys and brilliant) and one deracinated

cat— a Siamese of sorts. Tom loves them
all. They sleep tiered into corners, cribs, across
         your
bed at night, on kitchen counters, against the
         bathroom
wall— snoring, flatulent. The house does reek
with all this love; the babies cry; two dogs have

eaten another of Tom's toupees. (He hides that
         baldness
from the world, anyway, less well, you have
         decided, than he
hides— What?) You search the cookbooks for
cuisine, exotic and nostalgic fare; your dog-eared
         Becketts,
Sartres, and Camuses are marred by drool, dog

scent or cereal. Mementoes of the travels (yours
         and
Tom's) gather new dust, while literary talk
         becomes
inaudible through cries and panting: "Irony is
         the
modern form," you say now, keeping your eyes
         from Tom—
who loves the tragic or the comic best, or else
         romance.

Nancy Van Veenan
VILLAGE WOMAN

Once pretty
her braids are grey
her teeth gone.
She smiles quickly though
shyly—that was always her way
She doesn't ask for what we haven't got on the shelves.
She's waistless and comfortable
beneath her flowered summer parky
the back and shoulders faded
from hours under rain, sun
tending fish nets, picking berries close to the ground.
She spends her days with her husband
setting, checking, cleaning, drying, mending nets,
cleaning fish
dashing down river in the familysize boat
wolf rim to the wind
looking straight ahead as they go
to check their potato garden down there
or the caribou crossing by the graveyard.

She looks older than her man
aged by childbearing
and the beatings of weather and work
family rearing, too
until the daughters are old enough
(not long)
to drip coffee, roast moose, keep the homefire burning,
    floors pinesolmopped
and a bit of wringerwasher wishing
to maintain the long lines of blue jeans, T-shirts, sheets
and one flowered parky.

She has one more baby
always one more
this one given to her by her sister.

Nancy Lord
SEARCHING FOR LIAM

Bundled in parkas and hats, the three of them stood by the side of
the road. Fireweed fluff, like an early snow, floated across from the
adjacent field; the little girls clapped at it, sometimes catching the white
fibers between their palms, more often sending the seed-bearing fluff
spiralling away upward. Apple, her too-large wool cap nearly eclipsing
her eyes, arched her head further and further back in an attempt to see
out from beneath it. Her round cheeks shone ruddily in the chill of the
morning air.

Mossy, the older by two years, tired of the game and kicked a loose
piece of asphalt away from the side of the road. She walked, tightrope
style, along the broken edge of the pavement, her arms flailed out for
an exaggerated show of balance.

Marla looked at her children, frowning. She turned away to stare
down the road, one hand tapping against the side of her thigh
impatiently. Her long red hair billowed out over her parka collar, half-
hiding the knapsack which she wore on her back. Below the knapsack
her parka was streaked with dried mud. Although she was a small
woman, her hip-thrusted stance on the side of the road suggested a
strength that, like that of the spindly alder tree, only springs back with
greater resilience when pushed aside.

When she heard a car approaching, she reached for Apple's hand and extended her other thumb.

*   *   *

"Oh, Marla," Ginger said, pressing her hands on either side of her nose. "Why? Where would he have gone?"

The two children sat on the edge of the couch, still dressed in their heavy clothes. Marla stood beside a window, looking at a painting on the wall. "New?"

"Marla!" Ginger scowled as she ran a cleaning rag through the flute she'd been playing. "That son-of-a-bitch. I just don't understand why you ever got mixed up with him."

Marla stepped back across the room. "You don't know, Ginger. You don't know anything about it." Her green eyes met her friend's, warning with their intensity that enough had been said, then moved past her to examine the oriental rug, the china cabinet, and the linen tablecloth in the adjoining room. "You could be living anywhere."

"Is he feeding him?" Ginger asked, snapping her flute case shut. "Does he know what he's doing? Jesus, Marla, I'm just concerned."

"He's got all the bottles and stuff. He took almost all the clothes. I'm not *really* worried," Marla said. She paused. "But I am worried, sometimes he's so weird . . . unpredictable. He forgets."

Ginger stood up, glancing at the children on the couch and wishing they'd sat somewhere else. Their clothes, like their active little hands, were never quite clean. That was unkind, she knew. They were good kids—well-behaved—and they were Marla's. "You've called the police, haven't you?"

"What would I tell the police?"

Ginger rolled her eyes. "Kidnapping! It's a federal offense."

Marla, mimicking, rolled her own eyes.

"Marla!"

"I'm sorry," Marla said quickly. "It's such a great look, that beseeching of heaven. I've always admired the way that you do it."

"Thanks," Ginger said, sarcastically. "Look, if you won't report it, I will." She picked up the phone next to the couch. "Mossy, would you run in the kitchen and get the phone book on the counter there?"

Marla sat down in the space vacated by her daughter and reached over to place her thumb squarely on one of the buttons in the phone's cradle. "He can't kidnap his own kid," she said.

Ginger held the phone receiver in the air, the earpiece pointed at Marla like a large disciplining finger. "What do you mean he can't? He just did."

"He's the father. A father can't kidnap his own kid. Not legally." Marla squeezed over to make room for Mossy, who had returned with the phone book. She took the book and flipped quickly through it.

69

"Look how fat this is getting." She shook her head.

Ginger put the phone down. "What do you want to do?"

Marla looked at her with surprise. "Find them, of course. Look for them."

"Where will you look? How do you know where to look?"

"I'll just drive around." Marla stood up. "Can I borrow your car?"

"I'll come with you," Ginger said. "Just wait for me to change."

It had to be a form of self-destruction, Ginger thought as she pulled a sweater over her head. There wasn't any other explanation for why Marla got involved with the men that she did. The relationships always ended in some kind of crisis. Of course, she mused, it was crises that Marla thrived on; they were what she expected, even wanted, in her everyday life. She'd seen the way Marla looked around her house—with neither envy nor contempt but merely wonder at such order, such stasis.

And yet, despite such vast differences between them, their friendship remained as firm as ever. Marla had been her best friend since third grade and still was her closest woman friend. Marla, her alter ego. When they were growing up, going through school, she'd used to think of the two of them as coming from opposing poles, pulling at each other with something akin to magnetic force, pulling each away from the extremity of her respective origins into some area of the center. Without Marla, she'd never have come to Alaska, for one thing.

*　　*　　*

Ginger drove, following Marla's directions. They headed through town first, checking the bars, the parking lots, the side streets, watching for the green Chevy pick-up with the cracked windshield. "Left," "right," "slow down,"—Marla gave the orders. Ginger did her best to follow, within the law. "I can't go in there," she said once, driving by an ordered turn. "It's one way."

"Go around then," Marla said irritably. "There's a bowling alley down there."

"I hate to ask," Ginger said, circling the block, "but why would he be at a bowling alley with a baby?"

"I have to look everywhere." Marla said it as though she spoke of a mission. As long as she fulfilled her mission, she seemed to say, she couldn't fail to find the truck, and the baby.

Ginger stopped in front of the bowling alley. "Why don't you go in? Ask if anyone's seen him?"

"Drive," Marla said. "They won't tell me, but they'll tell him, and then he'll know I'm looking for him."

"Don't you think he knows you're looking for him?"

Marla shrugged. "Drive."

As they crisscrossed back through town, Ginger couldn't help

70

thinking how absurd they looked— she behind her big glasses slowly steering the Saab through the streets, Marla's red hair flying from the open window as she twisted to peer up alleys and through fences, the kids in the back seat each adhered to a side window. "Keep your eyes peeled," Marla had instructed them, and each was making maximum contact with the window. Apple, she noticed in glancing over her shoulder, was licking the glass.

"I've never paid so much attention to town," Ginger said to break the silence. "I've never even been down some of these streets."

Although it was set amidst spectacular natural beauty, almost everything within the town was an eyesore. Litter on the side streets filled the gutters, the paper and plastic blowing about with each car's passage. The ugliness was greater than the litter, though, or the broken neon tubes, or the used car lots. It was an ugliness inherent in the process by which the place had grown up. Bars and cafes, each with its own ethnic variety of grease, had slipped in between residential log cabins. Later, the multinationals had sandwiched their gilded headquarters among the pawn shops and charity shelters; the latter offered some protection to the street people who might otherwise have frozen in the oil company doorways. The tourist shops all sold painted goldpans; northern lights over a snow-covered cabin was the favorite theme. Boom and bust, boom and bust—each cycle had left its monuments, and its skeletons. The last boom had been the pipeline construction, and the gaudy face that had been painted at the time—the quick, cheap flush of easy money—had long since peeled and sloughed, leaving only scars and some persistant scabs.

An unsteady pedestrian staggered against the car as they stood stopped at a red light, then pounded abusively on the hood before moving off. Ginger reached over and locked her door.

"Bars must not be open yet," Marla observed. "The poor man's out on the street." She waved her hand in front of her, taking in the varied street activity. "It's a microcosm of mid-morning America." Businessmen walked to meetings, housewives rushed to sales, loiterers stood smoking beside doorways; all of them routinely moved away from the drunk as he bore down the sidewalk. What must have been a late-season tourist couple turned to watch him. Ginger saw the woman look up at the corner street sign as if checking directions.

When they reached the far end of town without spotting the truck, Marla directed Ginger to drive on out the road. They crossed the railroad tracks and bumped along over the frost-heaved, broken macadam. Ginger was glad to have left town to face instead the frost-turned hills rising in front of them with the subtle ochre and sepia tones of a simpler world. She wondered what the kids in the back thought about all this—this chasing in so random a fashion over the countryside

searching for the family's pick-up. She didn't know how much Marla
had told them, or how much they instinctively knew. Actually, she
reflected, having been dragged around on various adventures and
through numerous personal relationships for all of their short lives, they
were probably well inured to it all.

"Next right," Marla said, and Ginger turned off onto a dirt road.
About a mile down the road, Marla told her to pull over past a
mailbox. Without saying anything, she got out and walked back to a
driveway, then disappeared into the trees. A few minutes later she
reappeared, running, and leapt excitedly into the car. "He's been here,"
she said, breathing hard.

"Great," Ginger said, "but do you mind telling me where we are?"

"Her name's Bonnie. She lives here. She's his girlfriend."

"Oh," Ginger said. "That makes sense. How come we didn't look
here first?"

Marla ignored her question. "You've got to be the scout," she said.

"The scout?" Ginger turned abruptly in her seat. "Jesus, Marla,
what is going on?"

"I want you to go up to the house and look in the windows. See if
you can see any baby stuff inside."

"Didn't you just do that?"

"No, I'm afraid that she'd see me, if she's there. I'd rather that she
saw you. You can pretend you're a census taker or something. I'll stay
out here by the road and hoot like an owl if anyone comes."

Ginger rolled her eyes. Marla was really getting into it, almost as
though she were enjoying it. "How do you know that he was here?"
she asked.

"Tire tracks," Marla said. "Move the car further down the road,
around that bend. Then walk back and down the driveway. We'll be in
the woods." She got out and held the seat for the two girls to climb
out after her. Like a spruce hen, she swept her chicks before her into
the trees.

*　　*　　*

Ginger looked at the tire tracks as she walked down the driveway
towards the house. They were wide, like a truck tire, but she didn't see
any particularly distinguishing feature that would have convinced Marla
that it was Roger's truck.

She felt silly, doing this, spying on someone.

The house was typical of those found scattered throughout the woods
on the outskirts of town. It was owner-built, with odd angles and
unfinished sections. The plywood front above a story of log walls was
weather-stained, indicating several years of exposure to sun and rain.
Remaining building materials lay stacked in one corner of the yard,
partially covered with a brown tarp. A greenhouse, some of its plastic

panels missing, leaned against the south wall, and an unkempt garden, with some cabbages and what looked like Brussels sprouts still fighting the frosts, filled the side yard.

Ginger stood just within the trees, watching the house, and listening. There was no smoke coming from the chimney. There was no noise, and she couldn't see any movement within the dark windows. Using the trees as cover, she moved around to the side. She wondered what she would say if someone came out and asked her what she was doing, and she decided then to walk boldly up to the house. These people, some of them, shoot first and ask questions later.

She walked up and, standing on her tiptoes, peered into a front window. It was a living room, spare and orderly. A couch was covered with a blanket, several magazines were stacked on a coffee table. Two matched vinyl armchairs faced a black television screen. An art poster, showing a French train, and a leather-faced Eskimo mask hung on the back wall.

No clues.

Ginger climbed the cinder blocks which served as front steps and knocked on the door. She knocked again, louder. She turned the knob, just to check, and the door opened. Listening one last time for an owl's hoot, she crept in and circled quickly through the house. The kitchen was as neat as the living room, with a single coffee cup in the sink. Some clothes lay stacked on top of the dryer; none of them were baby things. She stepped carefully over the vacuum cleaner on the dining room floor and headed back to the door. Outside, she walked quickly away, her heart thumping in her chest. She felt guilty, as though she'd not only invaded a stranger's privacy but stolen some part of that person's self, a self defined by furniture arrangements and a fondness for cast iron pans. The tea kettle on the stove had been exactly the brand and color of her own.

She met Marla and the girls at the end of the driveway. "No one's there," she said. "There's no baby things." Marla looked crestfallen. "I even went inside," she added, knowing that Marla would be impressed by her daring. "There was nothing. There was just one coffee mug in the sink."

"You went upstairs?" Marla asked.

"No," Ginger said, defensively. Shit, she wasn't going to sneak through someone's bedroom, and get trapped under the bed when the owner came home.

"Then how do you know?" Marla's eyes flashed.

Ginger started walking towards the car. "Believe me," she said, "there was nothing."

As they got back into the car, Marla announced, "I've got another idea." She had Ginger drive back a short distance and park where they could watch the driveway. "This is what we do," she told the kids. "Whenever you hear a car coming, duck down so it looks like no one's here. They'll come back eventually, either him or her, or both of them, with Liam."

Ginger noticed that it was the first time she'd used the baby's name. If Marla'd asked her, she would have told her what she thought of the plan. It didn't make a whole lot of sense to her, staking out this place where Roger *might* have been. The woman was probably at work somewhere and wouldn't be home until dark. But then, just driving around didn't make a lot of sense either.

Traffic on the road was light, fortunately. Ginger quickly tired of ducking, particularly from behind the steering wheel. The kids loved it, though—waiting eagerly for the sound of a car, then diving into the upholstery. After each car passed, they'd shriek with the joy of their deception. It was a game to them, and Ginger wondered critically if Marla wasn't also enjoying the gamesmanship that she'd organized around the search.

Between shrieking sessions, Marla parceled out crackers and fruit to the girls. Ginger, alternating ducks with bites of an apple, wondered what the back seat would look like when they were done. It's for Liam, she kept telling herself. The only thing that matters is getting him back.

Although Marla might not show it, Ginger could tell that she was upset. When she looked sideways at her and she didn't know that she was being watched, her face appeared uncharacteristically drawn and pensive. Ginger thought that she detected an expression of regret.

The children, eventually tired out, curled up together and slept. The women continued their ducking, and talked of other things—movies, local politics, mutual acquaintances.

"Marla," Ginger asked at last, "you'll leave him when you get Liam back, won't you? For good?"

Marla laughed. "You never like my men."

Ginger stifled a sharp retort. Instead she asked, "Why do you have such a low self-image?" Marla made a face. "Seriously, Marla, I can't figure that out about you. You let men treat you like shit."

Marla made an exaggerated display of rolling her eyes. She pretended to take offense at Ginger's frown. "Hey, I'm just trying to perfect a useful mannerism. What makes you think I have a low self-image?"

"Just look at the men you've chosen." Ginger ticked them off on her hand. "Jeff, who got you pregnant and then disappeared. He was a loser from the word go. Andy was a real nice guy, but he didn't have

the brains of a muskox. Ed had all those war wounds, and the
flashbacks to go with them. At least he married you. Mike used to hit
you. Roger's a redneck, and a racist, not to mention his other sterling
qualities.''

Marla stared ahead out the window, the color rising in her face.
"Hey," she said, without looking at Ginger. "I didn't ask you to come
along. I only wanted to borrow your car. I'll take you home any time,
back to your sweet Professor Nicholas.''

"His name's Nick," Ginger said.

Marla turned towards her. "No offense, Ginger, but Nick's got to be
the most boring man I've ever met.''

Ginger felt her own anger rising. "Because he teaches? Because he
uses his head instead of stealing babies?''

"I said 'no offense.' I just said he was boring. He *is* boring.''

No offense! She should have known that Marla would come back
with something like that. She'd seen her do it with her men, too—the
offensively unoffensive counterattack, always with complete control.
Ginger snuck a look at her. Staring ahead down the road, Marla held
her chin up defiantly.

"Nick's been very good to me," Ginger said.

"That's what I mean," Marla said, after a minute.

"*What's* what you mean?''

"He's so good he's boring. I couldn't live with a man like that.''

Neither of them spoke for several minutes. The air in the car felt
close, and Ginger wrinkled her nose at the smell of urine. She cracked
her window and hoped that the smell didn't mean that Apple's diapers
had soaked through.

At last, Marla reached over and put a hand on Ginger's shoulder.
"Remember when we first came here—''

"Of course.''

"—and we danced in that topless place?''

Ginger snorted and shook her head. "I can't believe that was me. I'd
never have done it except that I didn't know a soul in the whole state,
so I couldn't be embarrassed. And, of course, you exerted your corrup-
ting influence on me.''

"Remember how alone we were, and yet how free we were—how the
world seemed so wide-open and full of opportunities? Every way we
turned there were new challenges.''

"I was always a little more apprehensive than you were. I admit, I
was scared some of the time.''

"Not me," Marla went on. "I'd never felt so alive, so—" she search-
ed for the word— "possible, in my life. Remember our first winter—
the ice fog, the union halls, the pipeline, the wild and reckless goldrush
mentality?" Ginger nodded. "We both fell in love with this country,

though I'm not sure that we loved the same things about it.''

Marla looked over her shoulder at the sleeping children before she spoke again. ''When I was working on the Slope, I did something once that I never told anyone about.'' Ginger waited. ''One day I just walked away from the camp, out into the middle of a blizzard. I knew that I could get lost, and die, but I wanted to do it. I *had* to do it. In fact, that one moment, that moment of standing in the blizzard, just before I turned back, was the most alive experience of my life. I was this close—'' she measured a fraction of an inch between her thumb and forefinger— ''of giving myself up to it. The wind was whipping by, I couldn't see or hear anything except snow and wind. It was probably a hundred below, with the chill factor. There I was, in the middle of the most hostile environment in the world, and I loved it. I knew that I could beat it, or I could give in to it, but that it was up to me. It was in my power.''

The two women looked at one another. ''This had something to do with Roger?'' Ginger asked.

Marla frowned. ''It was supposed to. I'm not always very good at getting a point across.''

''What was the point? Can't you just say it?''

Marla thought for a minute. ''You see, the thrill was going out in the blizzard, and knowing it could kill me. I could have just stayed in the camp, like everyone else.''

Ginger nodded slowly. ''I think I'm beginning to understand.'' It was a challenge, certainly, to stand up to the elements, or to an abusive man, to triumph over danger, the unknown, or the unpredictable. That was one explanation—meeting the challenge. But couldn't that be just a rationale for a masochistic nature, for always seeking out punishment? Surely no one wants a life of continual turmoil and hurt.

''That's why I live the way I do, too,'' Marla said. ''Cutting fireweed, hauling water, setting snares for rabbits. If I could live the way you do, I wouldn't. I'd die of boredom.''

''You'd have time to paint, to write, to throw yourself into other things.''

''No I wouldn't. I'd shrivel up into a crone and dissolve into dust.''

The light was already leaving the sky as the two women sat in silence. Ginger wondered whether she should be offended by Marla's derision of her own way of life. How boring I must be, she thought wryly, to play the flute when I could be splitting wood. How very unexciting.

''Do you have any idea,'' she asked at last, ''why Roger stole Liam?''

She thought that Marla tensed, but then realized that she'd simply startled her from whatever deep thoughts she'd been involved in.

''Yes,'' Marla answered.

''Why?''

"I threatened to leave him. I told him I was going to run away to At-
tu with the kids."

Ginger rolled her eyes. She couldn't help smiling. "Attu?"

"Yeah, I've never been there. There's no trees, and the wind blows
like crazy."

One of the children, stirring, made a purring sound.

"I don't think he's coming back here," Marla said. "Shall we go?"

*   *   *

In town again, they drove up one street and down the next, just as
they had that morning. Marla suddenly pointed to the truck, verdant
green above a surrounding sea of blue and white compacts. Without
talking, they turned into the lot and parked a few spaces away.

Marla got out and walked quickly to the truck, examining the con-
tents of the cab. Then she put a hand on the hood, testing for engine
warmth. With a glance, she surveyed the surrounding stores and
businesses.

When she returned to the car Marla rummaged in her knapsack for a
bandana and a pair of sunglasses. "Disguise," she explained, calmly. "I
don't want him to see me first." She covered her flaming hair with the
even redder bandana. "OK," she said. She pointed to the children, who
were now awake. "You guys hang tough. Stay here in the car. If you
see Roger, don't let him see you. Just watch where he goes." To Ginger
she said, "You take Penny's, I'll take the grocery. If you see him, come
get me; if you don't, meet back here.

Ginger watched the mud patch on the back of her parka as Marla
strode determinedly across the lot. There goes a woman, she thought,
who thinks nothing of lying in the mud to chain up a truck, even while
her man sits in the cab. Stiffly, she got out of the car and headed for
the department store.

Inside, she rode up to the top floor and began with the sheets and
towels department, circled through household, and came down to fur-
niture. In the jewelry section, sheer repulsion made her stop and ex-
amine the moose nugget earrings, bright with shellac. Quickly, she rush-
ed through the other departments, torn between wanting to find Roger
and hoping that she wouldn't. Marla hadn't said what her strategy was;
would she try to grab Liam away, reason with Roger, threaten to
scream or kick him?

Leaving the store, she hurried back to the lot. The truck was still
there; the kids hadn't seen anything. Ginger leaned against the side of
the car, watching for Marla; if she hadn't found him either she suppos-
ed they'd split up again and try some other stores. ·

Marla appeared then between two rows of cars, smiling, her bundled
baby held closely in her arms. Roger—big, beefy, bearded Roger with
his greasy hair falling across his eyes—walked behind her, balancing a

77

bag of groceries on top of a case of beer. He lumbered along, with a slow, bouncing gait that made Ginger think of a tame gorilla. If he hadn't been supporting the beer with it, she knew that his belly would be leading the bounce. Ugh. She looked back at Marla and kept her eyes on her face, waiting for the Madonna-like smile to break. Marla had removed both her scarf and her glasses, and she stared straight back at Ginger as she approached.

The two of them, Ginger realized with disgust, might from appearances be any all-American couple returning from a trip to the market, heading home to potato chips and beer. The burly husband, the pert little wife with babe in arms—they looked as though they might stop at any moment and hype a new chip flavor for a commercial.

Marla's smile stuck even as Ginger raised her eyebrows questioningly. "Well?" she asked.

Marla pulled a corner of blue blanket aside and showed her the sleeping baby's face. "I invited him to Attu, too," she said quietly. "He's going to build the wind generator."

Roger rested his load on the car's fender. "Hi, Ginger," he said. "How ya doin'?"

Ginger stared back coldly. Not a touch of embarrassment or shame was evident in his expression—just jocular good-nature, as though they'd met completely by accident in the course of their normal lives. She restrained herself from cursing at him and instead spit out a sullen "OK." Roger didn't seem to notice her lack of enthusiasm in greeting him.

Marla opened the passenger door and the children spilled out. "Thanks," she said.

Ginger was still trying to control her anger. She looked at a bird dropping on the roof of the car. "Anytime."

The children called goodbyes and she answered automatically as they skipped away. With her back against the door of the car, she let her eyes wander over the edges of the surrounding buildings, darkening before a back-lit sky. Their right angles, which sharpened as she brought them into focus, were somehow comforting.

She heard the truck start up, then pull out and move past her. As it idled at the exit, she sighed heavily, feeling weighted with defeat, and turned to look at it. Apple was waving frantically through the back window. Marla's face was in profile, and she could see her mouth moving as she talked to Roger. Then she, too, looked back. Although her lips continued to move, her eyes, catching Ginger's, rolled dramatically. Ginger laughed and raised a hand to wave. Somewhere inside, something loosened and stretched, and she knew that she'd slid more towards the center.

Sheila Nickerson
HISTORIES

I have walked some years now
through this land of histories—
sisters, aunts, brothers,
cousins, mothers, fathers—
and am left with this for a map:
there was someone we loved.
She hurt us. She went away.
She was returning. We assembled
her mail, all good, around her
place at the table with pink
sweet peas, her favorite, to
await her arrival. She never
came, though August did with
years of bright sweet peas.
Whether disease, crash, or crime,
we wait. Her place at the table
gathers shadows but cannot be reset.
A capital city on the map of our
memories, its smokes reach out—
bright red and unerasable—
to hold down space.

Gloria Bromberg
AFTER EVY'S FUNERAL

Safeway,
in the meat section, yards
of dark slabs, pale
chicken parts, small round
containers of giblets, hearts,
livers. Dungeness crab,
deveined prawns,
hog's maws.

My hands get colder. I lift
packs of ground beef, black-
red juice dripping
from the wrapper.

An old Eskimo woman
compares perch. Over-
whelmed by her parka:
flounce traveling down
thighs to knees, hem
and sleeves trimmed in embroidered
ribbon, all sewn together in
lush, green corduroy.

She looks up; her eyes
lock with mine. She smiles
a broad, broken-toothed
smile, the wolf ruff
blazing like a corona
around her weathered face,
a face broken into a million
thin, floating lines when she smiled,
looked right at me,
right into my eyes.

I smiled back
and I cried.

Jean Anderson
CAROL

Carol, your broken forearm
healed like a scythe, that curve of bone
reborn to crystalize the sweep of your
forgiveness: How
we watched your mother ("Crazy
as a loon," the neighbors said) dance
in the traffic island — fat, holding that
string grocery sack, a veiled hat
square on her uncombed head, and both socks
rolled to meet her old and broken
sandals. How

you told me then your Daddy'd promised
never to sign her in again, because she'd
cried and cried and begged and begged him
not to. How
you said that nothing was because she was a
woman born so poor. Nothing
caused by being Jewish (in the '40s) — big
and ugly, too— but simply: "Chance." Just
"chance" you said, and wept and ran away
before she saw us see her there and
dancing. How

you told me that when the menstrual blood
came (yours so far ahead of mine), it
could not be one's own. "Not
mine," you said the day it came,
"because it's woman's blood. It
births the world," you said. "It is
the world's blood." And you smiled sadly,
radiantly, Carol.

Mary TallMountain
SOALT'IN TLEEYAGA

Sitsoo
Grandmother,
In lamp-light
Biting sinew with gleam of teeth.
Grandmother,
My mountain Grandmother.

Small aunt, I hear you
Talk in falling leaves
Of dying summer,
Hands outstretched
While the women chant
For mother,
Suspended alone,
Harshly breathing Yukon wind.

"Tend for me your father," you say,
Mother your words
Misty as rain on the river.
I tell you—
I will walk in your shoes.
You and he will soon embrace
My two brothers. Ahhh,
I want to sing
How Soogha would build a sled,
How Kitl'aa would play to us
Music for a night of snow.

Soalt'in tleeyaga,
Indian women,
You, my other selves,
Through my every feathered pore
Your bright spirits
Inhabit my present shape.
Lead the way
O into the light.

Soalt'in tleeyaga = Indian women
Sitsoo = my grandmother
soogha = my big brother
kitl'aa = my small brother

Mary TallMountain

NAAHOLOOYAH

Nobody's hands were quite like Mamma's. They were narrow with long thin fingers, and thumbs that bent out at the ends. The nails were scarred with nicks from the cutting of Salmon. In fish time they had rims of black which had faded by winter till they were their usual pink-brown color. When Mamma rested they folded, one on top of the other and it seemed as if they were sleeping, but they were always ready to jump up. When they did, the turned-out thumbs gave them a busy air. The skin of her hands was both soft and rough. The girl thought about Mamma's hands coming toward her and Michael, usually holding things. It made her drowsy and comfortable.

At fish camp she had spent hours watching those hands work.

The right hand sailed clear up over the mother Salmon's big grey and pink body to her head, where it made two short strong chops with the sharp *t'laamaas* that made Salmon's head slide away on the slippery table. From then on, how fast it moved! Every move was important. First, the two upper fins were flipped away and the lower one was sheared off low on the pearly breast over the sweeping fan of the tail. Next, Mamma's hand lifted and *t'laamaas* drew a long red stroke that opened Salmon's belly. There in her silver lining were the perfect little jelly-red eggs. Ever so slowly, the right hand pried out the clump of

eggs. Not much else was there, because Salmon ate hardly anything
when she was going home with her eggs, that Mamma said were baby
Salmon. Now the right hand ran *t'laamaas* in another quick red line
along the ivory colored backbone. Both hands pressed the two halves
out flat. They picked up *t'laamaas* again and made slanting slices out
from the thick inner body almost to the thin outer edges. These cuts
were so fine that the skin was still all whole and was one skin, and its
inside was red velvet. There was the fresh smell of new fish, the smell
that Lidwynne thought she had always remembered from some dark
place inside. It was a good smell and made her saliva bubble up. She
thought she would like to taste a piece of that beautiful red velvet, right
now.

When Mamma cut Salmon, the hands acted more careful than they
ever did. It took both of them to dip Salmon into the tub of water and
hoist the two halves up to hang over the drying rack. Lidwynne kept
thinking now about the full racks of red king Salmon, and the taste
buds puckered more strongly. She could almost taste the sweet smoky
fish, the oil that was being heated out by the sun. How heavy *t'laamaas*
was, how the Salmon's body pushed back at the sharp blade, but always
gave and divided under it. Someday, she intended to cut Salmon herself.
By the time she got to be ten, maybe even nine, Mamma would let her
do it. Her hands would be big enough then, but now they were too
small. Most Salmon were as big as she was. Much bigger than Michael,
she thought.

He was grinning at her, with one tooth missing. It made him look
wild and cockeyed. A blue sweater peeked out under his wadded and
patched overalls that had once belonged to Lidwynne. "Where *eenaa*?"
he asked. The wind gently rumpled his curls.

"In the house, Michael." She looked up at the window. Nobody was
there. She had been upset, these days. Mamma and Daddy Clem had
talked a lot, secretly. She was sleepy and lazy now because she'd lain
awake so long trying to hear what they said. Mamma was very tired,
too. Scary things had happened yesterday: first the soldiers fighting here
in the yard, then Sister coming to see Mamma, her heavy black veil over
her face that frowned. It seemed that all over the village, people were
mad.

Mamma came outdoors. It was the first time since lunch that she had
been out to see what was going on. Lidwynne was kneeling by
naaholooyah now. There was a row of three, each with its little skin
roof. The clayey dirt had got dry, and the flaked mounds of the walls
were pale brown the color of pancakes. She pointed. "Look at
naaholooyah!"

"*Snaa'*, you make dandy winter houses." Mamma sat down with her
on the hard-packed ground.

"Maybe we go to Kaiyuh this winter and live in *naaholooyah*," Lidwynne said, excited inside at the thought. She had never been to Kaiyuh to winter camp. Sometimes Mamma and Grandpa and uncle and aunt and their children went out there to the old hunting grounds. It was supposed to be a wonderful place.

"Mmm-hmm." Mamma's face had gotten serious.

"But you said we could!" Lidwynne cried.

"I said maybe, you little dickens!" Mamma grabbed her and carried her over to the boardwalk. Michael was rolling around on it, giggling. Suddenly he tumbled off into the soft grass. Mamma gave a big laugh and picked him up so he wouldn't get scared, but he squirmed and squealed, unusually cross.

Lidwynne complained, "Why didn't you come see *naaholooyah*? I called but you didn't listen."

Mamma's lips moved against her cheek. "There's no time. Too much visiting." She yawned.

"Why do they all come here and visit?" Lidwynne frowned.

"It's just one of those times." Mamma carried them into the cabin and put them down. When she poured milk into a pan to heat, Michael wrinkled up to cry. She laid him slanty on her lap and pried open his mouth. "There's a new tooth coming," she said. Lidwynne craned her neck. *Baghu'*, Mamma said, showing her the new tooth poking up.

"*Baghu'*," Lidwynne repeated. "When I was four did I have those growing too?"

"Sure, and you were cranky too, like he is right now."

"I was?"

"Oh, you're a cranky little girl." Mamma grinned into her eyes. "You're just like Grandpa. Look there."

Lidwynne stared at herself in the looking glass. She didn't think she looked at all like Grandpa. She was so short and he was so tall.

"See? Short and wide, like him. And you sure have got his temper." Mamma's dimple showed.

Michael sucked loudly at his bottle. "He's not mad any more. Look at that. He was plenty mad today, though. He bawled a lot." Lidwynne patted his warm little forehead. Now that he's four, she thought, he ought to eat regular food like I do. Not just that milk. Doctor Harry got mad when she wouldn't drink milk. She didn't like it at all. Maybe if she ever went Outside, she would get to drink real cow's milk. Now they just drank canned Carnation milk, mixed with water. Mamma and Nellie had to talk real hard to get her to drink it at all, but Michael never got tired of it. His face smoothed out now, and his eyelids kept shutting. His arms dropped back and his mouth slipped off the bottle. Mamma laid him in *ts'ibil*. "You can cover him up," she said.

Ts'ibil was a shallow pouch of heavy, well worn canvas a yard square, hung from the ceiling by four solidly braided ropes passed through a fat gray coil spring and made into a ball-shaped knot, from which they splayed out to the corners of the frame and looped under the hard wide lip of wood over the edge of which the canvas curved up tightly; precisely spaced, the ropes wrapped around and under the lip and were nailed with the edge of the canvas to the smooth bottom. It was a sturdy smooth bowl deep enough to hold Michael safely. A nudge of the hand set the spring dancing lightly to put him to sleep; a harder one set it bouncing fast enough to awaken him without frightening him. Uncle Obal had made it. Lidwynne was going to have one too, when she had babies herself. She never missed a chance to watch Michael sleeping. Then she gently rocked him in *ts'ibil*. But she was too excited to sit still today. She pulled up the marten fur blanket and tucked it solidly around him.

Mamma sat down in her rocking chair by the window. "Hand me my thimble," she said. It was a regular thing they did, and Lidwynne gave her the thimble, which was a piece of caribou horn, shaved thin and curled to fit Mamma's thumb. Mamma threaded a needle with the papery thin *tl'aah* made of reindeer sinew she used for sewing hides. The *tl'aah* was tough, all right. Those hides were strong. Lidwynne watched her mother intently. Piles of *yoo'yoo'*, pink, silver and blood-colored, gleamed in the fat sunbeam that dangled across the room. Those long fingers picked up a pink bead on the very end of the needle and stiched it to the piece of moosehide in her lap.

"Some day Lidwynne's going to do that." She leaned on the arm of the rocker. "That's going to be mittens," she announced. "Mittens for Lidwynne this winter."

"Yes," Mamma sighed. That thinking look was in her face again. "For Lidwynne this winter."

"What's the matter?" Lidwynne looked into Mamma's face that was bent over the beads, so bright in her brown hands.

Mamma looked at her. "*Snaa'*," she said, lingering over the word. There was something different in the tone of her voice today. "I have to take you and Michael to stay with Doctor and Nellie."

"What for?" Lidwynne thought: Again? it must be a joke.

"I'm going to be too busy to keep you this week."

"What you have to do?"

"I have to be ready if Grandpa calls me to council meeting."

Lidwynne's face brightened. She wasn't going away this time.

"Council meeting are about you and Michael."

"Why? What did we do?"

"Nellie and Doctor asked me if they could adopt you. You know that."

Oh, that crazy adoption stuff, again. "That what Grandpa was so mad about yesterday?"

"Mm-hmm."

"You mean you want to give Michael and me to them?"

Mamma looked out the window. The wind had started to blow in the grass, and the river was all rough. "Yes," she said.

Lidwynne's eyes got hot and trembly. "Why do you want to do that, Mamma?"

"Oh, *snaa'*, I don't want to." The last two words sounded heavy through her nose. But she went on talking in that funny sounding voice. "It's because I'm sick. That's the reason I have to let them keep you kids so much. They can take care of you better."

It wasn't a joke at all, then. Suddenly Lidwynne remembered Mamma coughing this summer, even when it was hot weather. And how when she laid her cheek on Mamma's chest she heard little whispers in there. She had thought before that it was just the way she breathed. Was that part of this sickness she was talking about? "They want to keep us all the time? At night and everything?"

"Yes, that's right." Mamma kept her face down looking at *yoo'yoo'*. Why won't she look at me? Lidwynne thought, putting her hands on Mamma's face. She turned around then to look out of the window, and it felt like she'd gone a long way off.

Real fast, Lidwynne hugged her. "You love me?"

Mamma made a deep chest sound and began to cough. Lidwynne got one of her big white handkerchiefs and Mamma blew her nose. She stared into Lidwynne's eyes, and now she was back from wherever she'd gone. "Of course I love you, foolish little one. I don't want you to go away. But if you do, I know you'll have a nice life, the way Doctor and Nellie do."

"Grandpa won't let them have us."

"He hasn't got anything to say about it. He just makes sure council does everything right. They have to decide. He stays with them till they do." Mamma snipped off a little thread close to the knot she'd made in back of the mitten. She put the skins away and closed the box. Everything in the room got clear and sharp like Lidwynne's reflection in the mirror. She would never forget *yoo'yoo'* burning like fire in the sunbeam.

She flung her arms around Mamma. She wanted to hold her so hard that she couldn't get away from her, ever. "I don't want to go any place, not even with Michael. I want to stay here."

"Ah," Mamma said to herself. She nuzzled her face into Lidwynne's neck. Her breath was warm on Lidwynne's skin, and her words made puffs of damp air, tight against the little wrinkles of fat under her chin. "I want you to stay, too."

"But why do we have to leave you? Can't we just visit them like we visit Auntie Madeline?" Lidwynne moved away and stared into Mamma's huge eyes the color of shining blackberries.

"Now, I told you I'm sick. We can't help that. It's just lucky Merricks are here. You've already told me you like them. If you don't, why do you want to go there visiting all the time?" Mamma's words sounded like echoes of themselves in a big dark cave.

Lidwynne knew her lower lip was beginning to stick out. It was getting colder in here. It must be the wind. She kept silent.

"They're good to you. They love you, Lidwynne. Don't you see, after a while I'll get sicker." Her rough hands came up and held Lidwynne's cheeks tight, and she saw her own relections like dark still twins in Mamma's eyes.

"You're never going to get well?" Tears jumped out of her own eyes. Mamma wiped them. Then her face was buried in Mamma's apron and the hands were on her hair, patting, patting.

"Lidwynne, remember this word. Consumption. Your mamma had consumption, and she can't get well."

"It's terrible, to hurt you," Lidwynne sobbed, throwing her arms around Mamma's legs, hugging. The hands kept patting. Mamma rocked gently, and it was quiet in the room except for the little squeak of the rocker.

"Hey, *snaa'*, remember how mad Grandpa was yesterday, jumping all around?" Mamma was shaking a little. She must be laughing. Lidwynne peeded. Mamma was all dimpled up and her eyes were squeezed shut. She hollered, "Hoh, hoh! that funny Grandpa!" Lidwynne started to think of Grandpa and how he had looked. His face was red, his eyebrows were squeezed down into a white fringe so you couldn't see his pupils, and oh how mad he was, just yelling and yelling. Pretty soon she was laughing too, and they laughed till they were so tired they couldn't laugh any more, and they were hugging and kissing, and Mamma wiped their faced and rocked her a while. Squeak, squeak, that's all that you could hear, and the two of them there warm and cozy in the quiet place.

Suddenly Lidwynne sat straight up. "Why can't we live at the barracks with Daddy?"

"He works for Uncle Sam, and he's got to go to Fort Gibbon pretty soon because Uncle Sam needs him there."

"Oh, that Uncle Sam!" Lidwynne filled the granite dipper at the water pail. She gulped the fresh river water, trying to swallow something that seemed to have gotten stuck in her throat.

She stared out the window. The wind had grown so strong it roared around the trees, stirring them up as if it had a spoon a big as a cloud. It whined over the roof and down the stovepipe and teased the fire so it flickered fast as red devils back of the little flower-shaped vents in the firebox of the stove. Its voice was like lots of people singing, far away.

It had blown *naaholooyah* away. There were only three small brown circles left on the ground.

t'laamaas = woman's fish knife
eenaa = my mother
snaa' = my child
naaholooyah = winter house (underground, old style)
baghu' = his teeth
ts'ibil = baby swing
tl'aah = sinew (thread)
yoo'yoo' = beads

Karen Randlev
THE OLD WOMAN
AND THE ICE CAVE

The old woman watched
the winter wind
from her window
and lit the seal oil lamp,
shielding the flame with her cupped hand
until the wick caught
and filled the room with sweet smell
and light.

Outside
the wind blew
too hard for even the strongest
hunter to walk along; nanook
crouched beside the ice floe and waited;
earth was quiet except
for the spirit breath of the wind.

Still the old woman watched.
She knew she must wait and watch,
but not ask, for Telulijuk — spirit
of the sea — was restless.

As the old woman watched,
Telulijuk raged and blew,
the winds of her anger billowing out
to churn up even the sea
beneath the ice cover.

But the old woman could only wait
and watch, so powerful was the force
of this spirit.

Suddenly the lamp light of the old woman
flickered
and died as the wind
became stronger — the spirit's breath pushing
through each crack of the house
until
the very beams of driftwood
beneath the sod roof
creaked and groaned
until
the old woman could stand it no longer.

Quickly pulling her atigi
over her head
and grabbing an old caribou bone,
she opened the door
against the howling
dark of night.

Calling to Telulijuk,
the old woman said,
"Stop this wind,
spirit from the sea. I bow to your power,
but I must stop you
before my house is destroyed
by your spite and rage."

For a few star seconds, the wind
stopped, as if Telulijuk were thinking
about what her earth sister had said.

The old woman cried out again,
"Stop, spirit. You have done enough.
The sea is raging, the wind is a knife
cutting into the darkness. Enough."

But to Telulijuk, her sister's words were not
to be heeded. The old woman had no right to say
"enough."
Only the spirit herself could know
and with a defiant push, she blew
so hard that the ice shattered
into sheets along the shore.

But this old woman was very stubborn.
With the energy of her youngest grandchild,
she raced to the beach cliffs. Raising
high the thigh bone of the caribou, she shook
her anger towards the sky.

And still the wind blew.
So she shook again.
And still the wind blew.

The third time, before shaking her earthly rage
at this arrogant spirit, the old woman
bent over, peering into the night, to see
if Telulijuk were listening.

At that very moment, the great spirit of the sea,
Telulijuk, with every bit of her rage and power,
clapped her hands
like the willow wands on the skin drums
and changed the old woman
into an ice cave
where she would remain
until the days without nights
returned with their warmth
and carried this ice
out into the sea.

Joanne Townsend
FRIEND

Rain on Tuesday.
Rain on Wednesday.
Rain on Thursday.

You leave your warm house
overflowing with rabbits, dog,
children, toys, books,
tasks begging to be done,
to show me your city,
anxious lest I miss a single sight.
Wipers work like sturdy horses,
even hands must keep rubbing
steam from car glass
to frame the space
from which I view.

Flying home, the pilot
points out Hope, Alaska,
I look down on a village
flooded with sun
and think of you,
how you move with grace
through those gray days of sameness,
making of your life
a palette of courage-colors.
The true rainbow is the heart.

Joanne Townsend
RUNNING FOR MARLENE

1

Alaskan shores are frozen.

In the dim convoluted recesses
of my mixed-up mind,
where men are not welcome,
where death is fenced off,
I'm running for you,
Marlene.

I'm running for you
on every beautiful beach
that ever was, is----
Along warmer, gentler shores,
my feet push down against the sand.
Fast, I'm running for you
and hard,
my feet trampling
sands you wished to sift between your fingers.
I'm running.
Grain by grain, between the cracks of my toes,
sand sticks
fixed in permanence.

Beyond the dunes, soft
winds weave tall grasses
into patterns, wavings.

Your hands wove tapestries.

2

We women poets
burn ourselves out too soon.
Those of us who made it
through our thirties
into our forties
face "special" problems.

We were born too late for decadence.
We were born too soon for psychedelia.
We no longer age well
like the indomitable Miss M. Moore,
wearing oxfords,
carrying the proper satchel.
(She was a spinster.)

Between sanity and insanity,
we balance along a thin rope.
We walk on it by our hands,
our hands weathering, holding
between sanity and insanity,
between creativity
and

The weakest link along our chain,
you were our sacrificial lamb,
this January.

Come another time,
death, that slick charlatan,
will present his warrant, postage-due----
for me
        and me
and
    me.

My fingers grip the narrow rope.
My hands chafe and burn.

Donna Mack
WINNING THE WOMEN'S RACE

Not a hour ago it was so exciting. I was so excited I'd started out way too fast, and now my face was hot and my feet burned and there was that other pain. It had seemed so easy when Larry Ross spoke above the din of excited chatter, the starting gun raised above his head. "Fifteen seconds," he had said. "Fifteen seconds and the race will begin."

My daughter, Jamie, was a little ways ahead, looking all healthy and young, while all around there heaved a soft sweet sea of femininity, as women and girls of every size and shape and age prepared for the run. I remembered thinking that perhaps this one generous day of the year, even I could be a heroine.

It was a perfect day for running. Though the sun had been blazing for three days, now the sky was overcast. I didn't hear the starting gun go off, but it must have been at just that moment when Jamie turned around and smiled. Her hair was pulled back exposing a slight pulsing of excitement at the temple. The beginnings of breasts shadowed her shirt.

A brief lull in the congenial conversation was only now and again punctuated by shouts of encouragement from the husbands, fathers, lovers and sons that ringed the tract. Then Jamie turned away from me again, and there was a gradual lengthening in distance between us. I

96

burst ahead too fast, propelled by the excitement and not wanting to let her go.

One and a quarter times around the track we smiled and nodded, before zigzagging through the streets to where we began our descent down the bike trail. As Jamie's bright green shirt bobbed around a curve to become lost in the shining sea of hair and oiled arms and flashing knees, I realized how very much I wanted to run with her all the way. But I wasn't able to catch her, and I knew even if I somehow could, I would never be able to keep up.

The last thing I saw of her, she was lifting the hair from the nape of her neck with one hand, exposing that vulnerable sweet smelling curve. As a baby after her bath, I had nearly inhaled her through that spot and as she grew, I sniffed more carefully that unique odor that faded with the years. Of late I've been left selfishly guarding its memory or, once in a while when she drapes her lengthening limbs over the arm of the stuffed chair where I sit, indulging in a bit of odorous hallucination.

But now she had gone on ahead and here I was with my breath coming in gasps and my heart pounding. That small clean pain throbbed once again deep in my breast. Maybe I wasn't in good enough shape after all. He had said it wouldn't hurt anything to run. The wound he'd made was healing perfectly.

What was that up ahead a little ways? A cluster of people and a table. A friendly face attached to an arm reached out offering a glass of water. "You're half way through," she smiled. I kept my faltering pace while tipping back my head, more for the benefit of the onlookers than for any other reason. The water was good. What cool relief.

"Keep up the good work!" a professional looking lady called unruffled from the sidelines as she snapped shut the case of her camera. Why did she irritate me so? Was it because I was all red and flustered while she looked as though she didn't have a care in the world? Her face seemed vaguely familiar. Was she a photographer from the newspaper, still hanging around for some human interest story, while all her peers were recklessly racing to the finish line where the fastest runners were already coming in? Would anyone be there when I came in? Would I even make it? The bottoms of my feet burned.

Still, I kept on running. Maybe when I was out of that photographer's sight I'd walk for a while. That was the one thing during training I'd said I wouldn't do. I'd pledged to keep jogging even if to everyone else it loked like a loping walk. But now really, what difference did it make. I glanced back over my shoulder.

The photographer was grinning back at me! She waved! She hadn't taken my picture had she? That is just what I needed. I could see the headlines, "Middle Aged Housewife Makes Final Attempt to get in Shape" or "Housewife Drops with Exhaustion Trying to Stay Young."

Oh what was I doing out on this bike trail trying to run a race anyway? What was the use of it? Was there any reason for me to go on?

I shouldn't have let Jamie talk me into it. It was almost 6 weeks ago now since she pestered me while I sliced green wedges of avocado at the kitchen counter. "A mother and daughter team," she had said, but now I was left far behind. "You can do it Mom, it's all in fun," but now my legs felt heavy, my feet weighted. Finally I'd giggled shaking her shoulders, "Ok, Ok," I said. "Just don't expect any Chariots of Fire."

But that wasn't the only thing Jamie talked me into. I wasn't going to do the other either. Just two weeks ago, I came home from the doctor shaking my head. "No, it's nothing," I said, "I know it's nothing." But every time I shook my head or turned my face away, it was Jamie who insisted I look again. "You're probably right Mom, it's nothing," she told me over a steaming cup of red zinger one afternoon, as the Alaskan sun glanced hard off the surface of my kitchen table. "But it won't hurt anything to be sure."

"I have no curiosity about the matter at all," I said. "Why should I do it just to satisfy yours?"

But at night I tossed in bed, spinning my arguments like an old spider whose threads had grown too flimsy to catch flies. The evidence was too slim. The doctor was knife happy. It was some unjust payment for my mother's sins. If I hadn't told him about her, he never would have suspected anything.

Now was I leaving some awful legacy to Jamie?

From somewhere on Arctic Blvd. came the roar of a motorcycle. I searched the sound for the Raaaaaiiiiiinnnnnneeeeeeerrrrr Beeeeeeerrrrrrrr advertisement until it faded to the dull din of a swarm of insects. Mosquitoes. I shuddered. And then letting my imagination loose, considered once again that dark low cloud over Winchester Lagoon, this time coming to life, winding its way along the bike path, mingling with the scented flesh and pumping muscles. Were we all being chased by a cloud of thirsty humming mosquitoes?

"You can't joke it away," Jamie told me when I'd played the dying martyr, clutching my breast and gasping as I explained what the doctor would do.

But what did she know of the power of jokes? In all her realism what did she know of the back door of my mind that kept me going?

I felt strangely giddy, light-headed. Suddenly it occured to me that I had never run this far before. For an instant I was running into a dream. There seemed to be dots out there at the edge of my vision and someone's shadow just beyond my shoulder. In my ears throbbed the hard steady beat of my heart. And that cool illusive sensation at the back of my knees, it made me feel more like I was running away from something than towards the finish line. Quickly, I blotted the feeling away as I had blotted away the blood from Jamie's scrapes as a child with a damp washcloth, pretending they had never been.

Oddly, the face of that photographer floated once again into my mind. The shadow beyond my shoulder became her, stripped of her mocking self assuredness, joggling along in her high heeled shoes trying to stay up.

"Hello," I said. "So you've decided to join the race and find out what it's really all about, I see." My voice joggled up and down in time with my steps.

I was as surprised to be talking out loud, as the runner who just then jogged by. Her strides were strong and slow and easy. She drifted out around me glancing back with a look of puzzlement.

Now what was I doing? Talking to myself too? But the shadow over my shoulder, it still seemed to be there. I turned around and looked, squinting, trying to bring the black dots into focus. Then, I saw what they were. Swarms of mosquitoes in the brush off to the edge of the path. It was as if they were dogging me. There for a reason. But even though I knew what it was, I still had the sense of someone joggling along just out of the edge of my vision, trying to keep up.

Then I realized where I'd seen that photographer's face before. She *did* work for the newspaper. Each morning she'd smiled out at me from beside her column with my morning coffee.

I looked around at my surroundings. I had entered those unmapped swamps just before Lake Otis and a foul smelling steam rose all around. How different from that little manicured spot where she had stood, near parks and condominiums. Now *she* was having difficulty! How superior I pretended to be and the pain in my feet faded along with reality.

"I'm not going to run it all the way, I doubt if I could," she panted, leaning toward me with her microphone, straining to keep up. I loved making her subservient; strangely, *I* was experiencing an unexpected burst of energy. My legs soared weightlessly. Was it the competition of my invisible rival or could this be that much touted second wind I'd heard so much about?

There she was leaning towards me again, trying to speak, "But when I saw you, I knew I had to have an interview," she gasped. "The story of a real heroine."

I saw myself scantily clad on some science fiction poster, sword drawn ready for battle. "I am prepared to do battle!" I exclaimed.

Just then an Alaskan sized mosquito landed on my thigh and easily, I smashed the lethargic creature with the palm of my hand. Suddenly I saw the connection, I began to chuckle. Mosquitoes! Mosquitoes! I began to chuckle right out loud as I sailed along on some second wind, with mosquito smear on my thigh and the backs of my arms wobbling, talking to an invisible reporter while running a 6.2 mile race at my age

in my condition for crying out loud! Just when I'd thought I'd about
run out of juice, I realized I'd come to do battle.

"There is something going on here today you know nothing about." I
whispered. "A race beneath the race, one that only a select few runners
are even aware of. What luck for you that you happened to pick me." I
rubbed my hands together and chuckled again, picking the squished
mosquitoes daintily from my thigh where there was a vague streak of
my own blood.

"Did you know that the weight in tonnage of all the mosquitoes in
Alaska outweighs the combined tonnage of all the caribou herds?" I
asked, studying her face to see if she understood the full consequences
of my question.

"And that if an average sized man were staked out naked on the
North Slope, the mosquitoes would drain all the blood out of him in
thirty-five seconds?" I added, warming to the subject.

"Did you know each female mosquito lays 500 eggs, and they only
need blood on every eighteen generations? Now don't be deluded into
thinking this is good news. Think how many more of them this makes
possible!" I could see she was still confused.

"Do you have any idea the full consequences of laws that protect
Westchester Lagoon, Potter's Marsh and Goose Lake, not to mention
these unmapped swamps or low marshes in the war zone between UAA
and ACC?" A picture of the brilliant sunshine earlier this week warm-
ing sloughs of glistening mosquito eggs flashed briefly to my mind.

I loved this melodrama and began composing newspaper articles as I
hurried through this dark foul smelling region. "Here, phone this to
your editor."

Will the Human Race Survive?

(UPI) Anchorage Alaska   The June 7 Nordstrom woman's
race marks the pinnacle of humankind's struggle for survival.

According to geological, biological and anthropological data,
nearly one million years ago in the heart of the African conti-
nent, humankind began its evolutionary quest to populate the
earth. At approximately the same time, (geologically speaking)
in the swampy bowels of South America, mosquitoes began a
similar pursuit. Each species easily migrated and conquered un-
til they met in bloody battle some 50,000 years ago when each
was migrating to another continent by way of the Arctic Land
Bridge. After considerable losses on each side, both species,
weak from battle, gave up the fight and turned their attention
once again solely to survival.

Not until today, sports fans, did the mosquito feel secure
enough to launch another all-out surprise attack on over 1,000

Alaskan women very near the sight of their original encounter.

It is fitting that it be the human females who were attacked, for mosquitoes know it is mainly they who keep the embers of human kind glowing. It is also reported that mosquitoes are highly sexist, feeling human males would not be a worthy adversary. We must not forget that only female mosquitoes do battle and that males are viewed mainly as sex objects.

I could see by looking at her face that same mingling of dread and insight that had fallen to my stomach when I finished reading *One Hundred Years of Solitude*. In the end might it be that the world, in spite of all man's dreams and toil, really could belong to the insects?

This was great, I had spent a mile or more painlessly lost in my drama. "I have always had an unreasonable fear of mosquitoes," I went on. "Even as a child, like a foreboding, I shuddered as they drew away small red portions of my life, like time. But for all my mother's good advice, I got bitten anyway and swelled and scratched and got infected."

"Dab it with baking soda," my mother would say. "Don't scratch... Rub it with a dry bar of soap... meat tenderizer... vinegar... tea... ice..." My mother's words could just be heard under the sound of my own hard breathing...in the unsteady shuffling of my feet... "Don't use hand lotion, perfume, anything with a scent...Stay away from bright colors especially bright greens and blues...Don't go outside on cloudy days..."

I thought of Jamie far ahead being chased by mosquitoes in her new bright green tee shirt supplied by the sponsors of the race.

Now all the old discomforts were breaking through again, and there was a sharp pain in my side. I slowed down limping, closing my eyes trying to bring the reporter back.

As I entered the cool dark tunnel under Lake Otis, I caught tempting waifs of scented shampoos, herbal cream rinses and once in a while a hint of My Sin or Johnsons Baby Powder. The hollow exaggerated sound of my feet on the corrugated steel echoed my mother's practical advice, while the hard steady beat of my heart remembered truer fears.

It wasn't until I was driving home after the examination that the smile I had hid behind so faithfully made my face ache and the dark possibilities seeped into my being. He said I was in the high risk group and his eyes were soft.He said it would be a lipstick sized core, taken from just below the nipple; and he untied the kimono and touched me gently. I had smiled awkwardly when he told me his wife had lost her life to it. I had smiled awkwardly as I remembered my mother's own slow death.

A soft circle of light at the other end of the tunnel encased a beautiful portrait of the Chugach Range. I ran back into the day.

He took his lipstick sized core, but now he wanted just a little more.

As I approached the playing field just beyond the Northern Lights tunnel, my second wind gave out entirely. I felt so alone. There were no bystanders there shouting encouragement, or reporters to be embarrassed in front of if I stopped. I didn't though. Instead I began slowly rocking from side to side exaggerating each step, struggling to keep it up. My hands hung heavy and I was aware of the tendons stretched across my shins and of the muscles binding my thighs to my hip sockets.

As I entered the shaded lane beyond the playing field, for a while the sun came out. The blazing light flashed on and off, on and off, as I pushed myself down the path. Then, it was all sunlight, hot beyond explanation. Each leaf and blade of grass stood out stark and other worldly glowing in a faint aura. The skin hung on my arms, old, and dry and wrinkled. Briefly there came to my mind the brightly lit airport at 4 a.m., going home to my mother's funeral. How I'd wanted to brush my teeth, to wash my face, to not go on.

Up ahead the asphalt path reached upward, climbing the overpass. I leaned into it pumping my arms as I had been told, but each breath only left me more desperate for air. A tiredness seeped into my bones, I hadn't experienced since childbirth.

Then, there was someone at my side, a woman older than me with a softness around the mouth and eyes. Perhaps, I wasn't running any more, I was getting back my breath, though I still seemed to be going forward. "Just a little bit more," she offered encouragingly. How beautiful she was with her greying hair and soft blue eyes. The curve of her neck made me think of Jamie, or my mother. For a moment it was as though time stood still.

Then I was at the top of the overpass. A light breeze picked up my hair giving for a brief instant a feeling of flight. For some reason, I felt sure then that I would make it.

On the downhill side, suddenly there was a flurry of signs stapled to posts and shubbery. "We love you Mountain Mommas!" they said and "Fast Ladies, you can do it!" I saw then that I wasn't alone. There were women and girls of every size, each finding her own way along the path. How beautiful we were! I felt love enough for all of them and I got the unreasonable feeling we were winning.

As I searched their faces, tanned and fair, young and old, I realized I was once more trying to find the reporter. I couldn't leave her as I had, stumbling along lost, gasping for breath. This time she was at my side with running shoes, keeping perfect pace. "We're getting them," I told her. "In our own way we're getting them."

Once again I imagined that dark low cloud over Winchester Lagoon had come to life and was winding its way along the bike path, mingling with the scented flesh and pumping muscles. But now things had changed. We were fighting back.

"Why even now," I assured her, speaking clearly into the mike, "hundreds of mosquitoes are being slapped from thighs and wiped out of eyes. Greedier ones," I went on, "are no doubt exploding with gluttony."

Words began falling with each step. I composed an update. Tired as I was, I was surprised at how easily the article fell into place. All the statistics took on new meaning.

Day of Reckoning Postponed

(UPI) Anchorage, Alaska Due to a brilliant hold off by the women of Alaska, mankind may survive yet a bit longer.

Humankind's most sophisticated computers after calculating 500 eggs per female mosquito multiplied by 17 generations each times the life span of each mosquitoe times the amount of bites inflicted at the June 7 battle, have produced some startling results.

According to these calculations September 15 will be the telling day. Humankind's only hope will be to stay inside behind well screened windows, preferably wrapped in mosquito netting. It is believed that on this day trillions of 18th generation mosquitoes will blacken the skies, strip leaves off the trees and destroy the Mat Valley potato crop in their frenzied search for blood.

Do not go outside under any circumstances. We repeat. Do not go outside. If we can all resolve to do just this one thing, it is believed that the mosquitoes will leave the Anchorage Bowl in a deafening din of frustration, and in frantic desperation migrate to the valleys beyond in search of blood.

Being unsuccessful in their attempt they will then plunge with a final gasp into the valley just beyond Flat Top Mountain. There tons of mosquito corpses will begin disintegration.

From that time forward, Anchorage will be known as the city of birds. Easy access to food will bring brilliant species from all over the world filling the city with song. Fishing will take on incredible new dimensions as the trout and salmon feed lazily on mosquitoes washed into the interlacing system of streams. Fat ducks will drop out of the sky onto Thanksgiving tables, while new species of tasty shrimp drift up onto the Homer Spit for easy gathering. It is even predicted that generations from now when the last known oil has been drained from the land, a field will be found in the valleys beyond Flat Top Mountain outdoing all the others. Geologists will report that it is suspected to be the last burial ground of the then extinct mosquito.

Was that the finish area up ahead? Had I really done it? Had I really tricked and prodded and willed my way to the finish? Had that reporter, and my daughter and those mosquitoes and my own determination, really seen me through? I was smiling.

I've been told that sometimes when one pushes to the edge of exhaustion or pain or imagination or joy, something can break. For a brief instant the true significance of the universe is revealed. I pressed my eyes shut tightly and in one last surge pushed myself through the finishing gate.

The cheers of one lone girl rose from the grass at the edge of the parking lot. "You made it, Mom! You made it!" When I opened my eyes there was Jamie with a piece of watermelon in one hand and a rind in the other. She was calling from the place on the grass where she had long been waiting.

Mary TallMountain
THERE IS NO WORD FOR GOODBYE

Sokoya, I said, looking through
    the net of wrinkles into
    wise black pools
    of her eyes.

What do you say in Athabascan
    when you leave each other?
    What is the word
    for goodbye?

A shade of feeling rippled
    the wind-tanned skin.
    Ah, nothing, she said,
    watching the river flash.

She looked at me close.
    We just say, *Tlaa*. That means,
    See you.
    We never leave each other.
    When does your mouth
    say goodbye to your heart?

She touched me light
    as a bluebell.
    You forget when you leave us,
    You're so small then.
    We don't use that word.

We always think you're coming back,
    but if you don't,
    we'll see you some place else.
    You understand.
    There is no word for goodbye.

Sokoya = Aunt (mother's sister)

CONTRIBUTORS

Jean Anderson, in 1982, won an Individual Artist's Grant from the Alaska State Council on the Arts in recognition of her work in fiction and poetry. She is a founding editor of the literary magazine *permafrost* and is coordinator of Fireweed Press' next project, a statewide short-story competition.

Gloria Bromberg, moved to Alaska in 1976 from New York. A founding editor of *permafrost*, she has taught college literature and writing classes, as well as English as a second language. In 1983, she entered Antioch University-San Francisco to study feminist therapy.

Ann Fox Chandonnet is the author of a chapbook; *The Wife and Other Poems*. Her poetry has been published widely in Alaska and other states, as well as in Canada. She currently writes for the *Anchorage Times*.

Patricia Frankish was one of ten winners in the 1980 Alaska State Council on the Arts statewide poetry contest. She lives in Fairbanks.

Linda Green is an itinerant public health nurse who lives in Anchorage and works throughout central Alaska. For five years she worked in the same capacity in Southeast Alaska, where she regularly travelled to several Tlingit Indian villages.

Cindy Hardy is a graduate student in creative writing at the University of Alaska-Fairbanks, where she has taught English and worked in the Upward Bound program. In 1982 and 1983, she coordinated the creative writing divisions at the Alaska State Fair.

Karen Kohout lives at Tozikakat Bush Camp, upriver from Tanana. There, spring through fall, she writes and teaches her young son Robin. For the past several years she has wintered in Central America.

Megan Lindholm graduated from Lathrop High School in Fairbanks and now lives in Roy, Washington. She is the author of *Harpy's Flight* (Ace, 1983) and its sequel *Windsinger* (Ace, 1984), both fantasies. Her recent work is predominantly science fiction and fantasy.

Nancy Lord lives each summer in Homer, where she works as a commercial fisher, and each winter in Juneau, where she works as a legislative aide.

Donna Mack lives each summer in Homer, where she operates the folk-art store Sol y Sombre, and each winter in Anchorage, where she writes and cares for daughter Sonja and son Benji. A former recipient of the National Endowment for the Arts creative writing fellowship, she has served as literary panelist for the Alaska State Council on the Arts.

Nancy McCleery is the author of a letterpress chapbook, *Night Muse*, from Uintah Press, Port Townsend, Washington. She was a 1979 recipient of an Individual Artist's Grant from the Alaska State Council on the Arts. In addition to teaching creative writing at Anchorage Community College, she is writing lyrics for an opera, *Marco Polo*.

Katherine McNamara has lived and worked as an educator and poet-in-the-schools in interior Alaska for a number of years. She is currently at work on a biography of the artist Frances Demientieff of Holy Cross. In 1980, she received an Individual Artist's Grant from the Alaska State Council on the Arts.

Patricia Monaghan is a graduate of West Anchorage High School and a resident of Fairbanks, where she teaches writing at Tanana Valley Community College. She is the author of *The Book of Goddesses and Heroines* (E.P. Dutton), a survey of female figures in world mythology.

Cheryl Morse lives in Sitka, where she teaches creative writing at Sheldon Jackson College. With her husband Stephen, she produces chapbooks (as *Orca Press*) and a literary magazine (*Orca*).

Sheila Nickerson, former Poet Laureate of the state, lives in Juneau and edits *Lemon Creek Gold*, a journal of prison literature. Her most recent book is *Writers in the Public Library* (The Shoe String Press, 1983), based on her work as poet-in-residence at the Alaska State Library.

Tina Parke-Sutherland works and teaches with the University of Alaska-Fairbanks. She has also taught Alaska Native students in Upward Bound and other enrichment programs. She and her husband Bill have recently co-authored a novel, untitled, and a son, Billy.

Karen Randlev spent most of the 1970's in Alaska, living in Tok and Barrow. In 1980 she moved to Berkeley, California, where she teaches high school English and writes poetry and reviews. She has worked as a poet-in-the-schools in both Alaska and California.

Linda Schandelmeier was born in Anchorage, where she was raised on a 160-acre homestead. In 1971 she earned her B.S. in biological sciences from the University in Fairbanks, where she still lives with husband Grant Matheke and daughter Lauren. Awards for her poetry include first prizes in the Midnight Sun Contest of the Academy of American Poets and in the Fejes Creative Writing Contest in Fairbanks.

Mary TallMountain is an Athabaskan Indian born in Nulato and raised in an adoptive white home Outside. In 1980 she rejoined her Alaskan relatives and has since been traveling frequently between her San Francisco home and Alaska.

Joanne Townsend moved to Anchorage in 1970; there she produced a book of poems, *Balancing Act* (Harpoon Press) and edited the journal *Harpoon*. Now teaching at the University of Arkansas in Fayetteville, where she is pursuing graduate studies in English and American literature, she is awaiting the 1984 publication of her chapbook *Leavetaking* (Intertext).

Nancy Van Veenan is a central Alaskan writer who has lived in Fairbanks and in Ambler. Her work has been published frequently in Alaskan publications.